The Minister's Handbook
of Dedications

The Minister's Handbook of Dedications

WILLIAM H. LEACH, EDITOR

Abingdon Press

NEW YORK NASHVILLE

SET UP, PRINTED, AND BOUND BY THE
PARTHENON PRESS, AT NASHVILLE,
TENNESSEE, UNITED STATES OF AMERICA

Preface

For some years *Church Management* has been collecting from its readers services and litanies of dedication, which have been created on a local church level to meet the needs of the moment. During these years the number of churches has expanded, and their programs—including building and interior adornment—have expanded. Not being able to find services to dedicate the various items added to their property, the ministers, working by themselves or with worship committees, created the new programs demanded.

From many issues of *Church Management*, I have brought together and classified the services which I think will help many churches in the future. Sometimes one will be found which will fit the exact needs. In many more instances the pages of this book will offer research material to help thinking churchmen to develop litanies of dedication which suit their situations.

WILLIAM H. LEACH

Contents

7

II. FURNISHINGS AND EQUIPMENT

I
BUILDING AND SITE

1. MEDLEY OF SCRIPTURE VERSES FOR A GROUND-BREAKING SERVICE [1]

(with minor alterations[2])

Every house is built by someone, but the builder of all things is God.	*Heb. 3:4*
Behold *we* are about to build a house for the name of the Lord our God, *to*	*II Chr. 2:4*
dedicate it to him. We look forward to a *house* whose builder and maker is	*Heb. 11:10*
God, *for* unless the Lord build the house, those who build it labor in vain.	*Ps. 127:1*
By wisdom a house is built, and by understanding it is established. The	*Prov. 24:3*
fear of the Lord is the beginning of wisdom, and knowledge of the Holy	*Prov. 9:10*
One provides understanding. Blessed	*II Chr. 2:12a, 14b*
be the Lord *who has provided us men trained to work* in bronze, iron, stone,	
and wood . . . and to execute any design that may be assigned to them for	*II Chr. 3:3*
the building of the house of the Lord.	
In whatever one builds on the foundation each man's work will be made	*I Cor. 3:12-13, 10b*
manifest, for time will declare it, and fire will test what sort of work each has done. *Therefore* let each man take care how he builds. *Let him with skill lay*	

[1] By Edward E. Chipman, minister, Sunset Hills Baptist Church, Omaha, Nebraska.

[2] Words in italics are additions or alterations.

13

the foundation and build upon it, remembering that we are fellow work-
men with God.

Behold, says the Lord God, I am
laying a foundation, a sure foundation.
And he who believes will not be hasty.
And I will make justice the line, and
righteousness the plummet. *So let
us build,* knowing that God's firm
foundation stands bearing this seal,
"The Lord knows those who are his,"
and, "Let everyone who names the
name of the Lord depart from iniquity."

Let us therefore build upon the
foundation of the apostles and prophets, Christ Jesus himself being the
chief cornerstone, in whom the whole
structure is joined together and grows
into a holy temple in the Lord. As
therefore you received Christ Jesus the
Lord, so live in him, built up in him
and established in faith.

According to the commission of
God given us, *so let us build,* remembering "they shall see who have never
been told, and they shall understand
who have never heard." *Let us therefore* have reason to be proud of our

Isa. 28:16-17

II Tim. 2:19

Eph. 2:20-22

Col. 2:6-7

I Cor. 3:10
Rom. 15:21, 17

I Cor. 3:11

14

work for God, *having laid* the foundation *in* Jesus Christ.

So, beloved, like living stones be yourselves built up into a spiritual house, to be a holy priesthood, to offer spiritual sacrifices acceptable to God through Jesus Christ. *Thus* build yourself up on your most holy faith, praying in the Holy Spirit, keeping yourselves in the love of God, waiting for the mercy of our Lord Jesus Christ unto eternal life.

I Pet. 2:5

Jude 20-21

2. GROUND-BREAKING SERVICE FOR A NEW CHURCH—I [3]

MINISTER: Dearly beloved, we are assembled to dedicate and break this ground for a new house for the worship of Almighty God, the God our fathers. Let us not doubt that he will favorably approve our godly purpose, and let us now invoke this blessing on this, our undertaking.

EXTEMPORE PRAYER: (*By the leader*)

SCRIPTURE LESSON: I Chr. 29:10-18. (*To be read respectively*)

MINISTER: Wherefore David blessed the Lord before all the congregation:

[3] As used in the Faxon-Kenmar Methodist Church, Williamsport, Pennsylvania; Fred A. Stiner, minister.

15

PEOPLE: And David said, Blessed be thou, Lord God of Israel our father, for ever and ever.

MINISTER: Thine, O Lord, is the greatness, and the power, and the glory, and the victory, and the majesty:

PEOPLE: For all that is in the heaven and in the earth is thine;

MINISTER: Thine is the kingdom, O Lord, and thou art exalted as head above all.

PEOPLE: Both riches and honour come to thee, and thou reignest over all;

MINISTER: And in thine hand is power and might; and in thine hand it is to make great, and to give strength unto all:

PEOPLE: Now therefore, our God, we thank thee, and praise thy glorious name.

MINISTER: But who am I, and what is my people, that we should be able to offer so willingly after this sort?

PEOPLE: For all things come of thee, and of thine own have we given thee.

MINISTER: For we are strangers before thee, and sojourners, as were our fathers:

PEOPLE: Our days in the earth are as a shadow, and there is none abiding.

MINISTER: O Lord our God, all this store that we have prepared to build thee an house for thy holy name cometh of thine hand, and is all thine own.

PEOPLE: I know also, my God, that thou triest the heart, and hast pleasure in uprightness.

MINISTER: As for me, in the uprightness of mine heart I have willingly offered all these things:

PEOPLE: And now have I seen with joy, thy people, which are present here to offer willingly unto thee.

MINISTER: O Lord God of Abraham, Isaac, and of Israel, our fathers, keep this for ever in the imagination of the thoughts of the heart of thy people, and prepare their hearts unto thee.

GLORIA PATRI: (*To be sung by all*)

MINISTER: To the glory of God our Father, whose peace passeth all understanding, and to the love of his Son, Jesus Christ our Lord, and to the fellowship and blessing of the Holy Spirit.

PEOPLE AND MINISTER (*in unison*): We dedicate and break this ground. (*Ground is to be broken with these words.*)

PEOPLE AND MINISTER (*in unison*): We the people of this congregation, and of this community, do now in the sight of God and in the presence of each other, make our vows and dedicate ourselves to the end that here there may be a sanctuary, hallowed as a place of sacred worship and thorough instruction of Almighty God. That this may be a church that will exalt the ministry of the open Bible with its faithful record of human life, its unfolding of the redeeming grace of God through Jesus Christ, its message of warning, comfort, inspiration, and hope; a church that will be constant service to God and man.

HYMNS: "Rise Up, O Men of God."

3. GROUND-BREAKING SERVICE FOR A NEW CHURCH—II [4]

SENTENCES

"Lord, thou hast been our dwelling place in all generations.

Before the mountains were brought forth, or ever thou hadst formed the earth and the world, even from everlasting to everlasting, thou art God. . . . Let thy work appear unto thy servants, and thy glory unto their children. And let the beauty of the Lord our God be upon us: and establish the work of our hands upon us; yea, the work of our hands establish thou it."—Ps. 90:1-2, 16, 17.

HYMN

The Church's one foundation
  Is Jesus Christ her Lord;
She is His new creation
  By water and the word:
From heaven He came and sought her
  To be His holy bride;
With His own blood He bought her,
  And for her life He died.

MESSAGE

"The earth is the Lord's and the fulness thereof; the world, and they that dwell therein." From the good earth our heavenly Father has ordained that resources for our needs shall come. Man was made from the dust of the earth and from it his food comes. On it he builds foundations for his home, his business buildings, his schools, his

[4] As used in Central Presbyterian Church, Fort Smith, Arkansas.

churches, and all the accessories of his life. Into its inner recesses his body returns as his spirit is called home to God who gave it.

We are called this day, in reverence before God, to begin a great new work by breaking this soil and preparing the way for a beautiful new sanctuary which shall be dedicated to the glory of God and consecrated to bringing the spirit of God to many generations which shall rise in the future. May this be a sacred and hallowed experience and may we say in our hearts as we break this earth, "The place whereon thou standest is holy ground." Establish thou the work of our hands upon us, O God, yea the work of our hands, establish thou it.

BREAKING OF THE GROUND

(*The chairman of the board or a member of the building committee may break the ground by turning a spade full of soil.*)

DOXOLOGY

Praise God from Whom all blessings flow;
Praise Him, all creatures here below;
Praise Him above, ye heavenly host;
Praise Father, Son, and Holy Ghost. AMEN.

PRAYER AND BENEDICTION

Our Father, as a city that is set on a hill cannot be hid, so we pray that this sanctuary which we shall erect here on this hill shall bear testimony to the fact that Christ is a living reality and that he is still the light of the world.

May its beauty and its churchly appearance say to those who pass this way, that a Christian congregation had faith in God to build to the glory of his kingdom, and may we let our light so shine before men that they seeing these good works, glorify our Father who is in heaven.

Now unto him who is able to do exceeding abundantly above all that we ask or think according to the power that worketh in us, unto him be glory in the church and in Christ Jesus throughout all ages, world without end. AMEN.

4. GROUND-BREAKING SERVICE FOR AN EDUCATIONAL BUILDING [5]

A formal processional moves from the auditorium to the ground-breaking location: minister, director of religious education, boy scouts, girl scouts with flags and insignia— all followed by the adult and the youth choirs in vestments.

When assembled at location the following program is followed:

a) Introductory remarks by the chairman of the building committee. The chairman then presents the architect and the building contractor—no remarks by either.

b) The chairman presents the spade to the minister who turns first spade of earth as representative of the entire church.

c) Then the minister presents the spade to the represent-

[5] As used in the Lakewood Presbyterian Church, Cleveland, Ohio; LeRoy Lawther, Minister.

ative of the women's association—she then to the representative of the young people of the church—each one making
suitable remarks.

d) Prayer, closing hymn, benediction.

SUGGESTED STATEMENT FOR EACH OF THE FOLLOWING TO MAKE
AS THEY BREAK GROUND

DIRECTOR OF RELIGIOUS EDUCATION: In order that boys and
girls can be taught the word of God; and led to accept
Jesus Christ as their Savior and be encouraged to seek
membership in his church; and, on behalf of all teachers
and parents of this congregation who strive to show
and teach the way of Christ to children and youth, I
turn this spade of earth that a building may be com-
menced which will provide additional facilities for
Christian education.

WOMEN'S REPRESENTATIVE: On behalf of all the women of
this church who, since its founding —————— years
ago, have labored to support its local and world-wide
program of teaching, healing, and preaching; and, also
on behalf of all the women of the present congregation
of the —————— Church who labor for Christ and
his church here and throughout the world, I turn this
shovel of earth that a building may be erected to the
glory of God and the service of mankind.

YOUNG PEOPLE'S REPRESENTATIVE: On behalf of the children and youth of this congregation and community
who gather here for instruction and Christian fellowship, and on behalf of those who will come after us,
I turn this shovel of earth that a building may be

21

erected which will more adequately serve this and coming generations of children and youth.

MINISTER: Almost ——————— years ago a small group of devoted Christian men and women organized the ——————— Church that they might have a place to worship God, where their children might learn about Jesus Christ and his way of life. In order to meet the growing needs of a rapidly growing community they have from time to time added to their facilities and enlarged their building. Today the congregation finds its present facilities wholly inadequate to meet the needs of the community and to answer the challenge presented to it.

Therefore, as the pastor of this church, in the name of the Father, Son, and Holy Spirit, I turn this spade of earth symbolizing the beginning of the erection of a new educational building which will enable the congregation to do a greater work and to serve Christ more effectively in our city and throughout the world.

CLOSING PRAYER

We thank thee, our Father, for the church which evermore has held aloft the torch of Christ making light the pathway of the world, for the program of religious education that has as its purpose the enlightenment of the minds and the enrichment of the souls of our boys and our girls.

May thy blessing rest upon what we have done here today and may the coming months see this work here begun carried to a successful completion.

We pray for the architect who has aided us and directed us thus far. May he be guided in carrying out the plans so carefully made that this building may be most suitable for meeting our needs and be usable for all our various groups.

We pray for the contractor who shall have direction of men doing the work that he may be guided of thee as he follows the plans already made that this building may be practical for the purposes for which it is intended and that every means possible for the safety and protection of those who shall use the building shall be taken.

We pray for the safety of the workers as they go about their work—may they realize that they are not just erecting a building of mortar and steel, but a building to be dedicated to the worship of God and the teaching of the truths of Jesus Christ.

We pray that this congregation, guided of thee, be united in this common cause, loyal to their responsibility and their opportunity, giving full co-operation.

May this building now to be built ever serve the high aims and purposes for which it is intended. AMEN.

5. PRAYERS FOR USE IN THE LAYING OF A CORNERSTONE [6]

CALL TO WORSHIP

Our help is in the name of the Lord, who made heaven and earth. Except the Lord build the house, they labor

[6] As used in Knox Presbyterian Church, Goderich, Ontario, Canada.

in vain that build it. Other foundation can no man lay than that is laid, which is Jesus Christ. Glory be to the Father, and to the Son, and to the Holy Spirit; as it was in the beginning, and ever shall be, world without end. AMEN.

PRAYER OF INVOCATION

O Lord, who art exalted above the heavens; look down in the abundance of thy goodness upon us assembled in this place upon which we purpose to build a temple for the spiritual worship which becomes thy holy name. Bless that which we do, that in all our works begun, continued, and ended in thee, we may glorify thy holy name, and finally by thy mercy obtain everlasting life, through Jesus Christ our Lord. AMEN.

INTRODUCTORY PRAYER FOR THE LAYING OF THE CORNERSTONE

O Lord Jesus Christ, Son of the living God, true cornerstone, immutable foundation; establish thou this stone which we plant in thy holy name; and do thou, who art the beginning and the end, in whom all things were created, vouchsafe thy presence that this our work, undertaken for thy service, may be carried on and perfected, to the praise and glory of thy holy name, who, with the Father and the Holy Spirit, livest and reignest, one God, world without end. AMEN.

LAYING OF THE CORNERSTONE

In the name of the Father, and of the Son, and of the Holy Spirit, we lay this cornerstone of a house to be erected under the name of —————— Church, and devoted to the worship of Almighty God. "Behold, I lay in Sion a chief corner stone, elect, precious: and he that believeth on him shall not be confounded."

In this place may the faith flourish, the fear of God, the love of the brethren. Here may the voice of prayer continually be heard, the voice of rejoicing and salvation, the voice of praise and invocation of God's most glorious and honorable name, the name of the Father, and of the Son, and of the Holy Spirit, henceforth and forever. AMEN.

PRAYER OF DEDICATION

Almighty and everlasting God, who hast built the living temple of thy church upon the foundation of the apostles and prophets, Jesus Christ himself being the chief cornerstone, we beseech thee to prosper this work of our hands, which we have undertaken for the up-building of thy kingdom and the glory of thy church; and to this end, do thou establish this stone which we now place in thy name. Blessed be thou, O Lord God, who hast put it into the hearts of thy servants to build a house in which thou mayest be worshiped, thy gospel preached, and thy holy sacraments administered for the comfort and salvation of men.

Be pleased to accept the humble offering of thy servants and fulfill the desires of their hearts. Shield and defend those who labor with their hands upon this building, that there be no hurt or loss of life, and grant unto them and all of us here present, thy heavenly grace, that our gifts and all our service may be sanctified, and we become in soul and body living temples of the Holy Spirit, and who taught us to pray, saying: Our Father which art in heaven, Hallowed be thy name. Thy kingdom come. Thy will be done in earth, as it is in heaven. Give us this day our daily bread. And forgive us our trespasses, as we forgive them that trespass against us. And lead us not into temptation, but deliver us from evil: For thine is the kingdom, and the power, and the glory, for ever. AMEN.

6. THE LAYING OF A CORNERSTONE

MINISTER: Behold, I lay thy stones with fair colours, and thy foundations with sapphires. And I will make thy windows of agates, and thy gates of carbuncles, and all thy borders with pleasant stones. And all thy children shall be taught of the Lord; and great shall be the peace of thy children. That our sons may be as plants grown up in their youth; that our daughters may be as corner stones, polished after the similitude of a palace.

He shall bring forth the headstone thereof with shoutings, crying, Grace, grace unto it.

Therefore, now to the end that these prospects and promises may be fulfilled to the people of this congregation and to their descendants, God the Father Almighty, maker of heaven and earth, Father of our Lord Jesus Christ, our Father who art in heaven,

PEOPLE: **In thy name we lay this cornerstone.**

MINISTER: Son of God, the only begotten of the Father, head of the body, which is the church; head over all things to the church, prophet, priest and king of thy people, who on the cross didst suffer for our sins, the just for the unjust, who ever liveth to make intercession for us,

PEOPLE: **In thy name we lay this cornerstone.**

MINISTER: God the Holy Ghost, proceeding from the Father and the Son, given to be our abiding teacher, sanctifier, and comforter; Lord and giver of life,

PEOPLE: **In thy name we lay this cornerstone.**

MINISTER: Holy, blessed, and glorious Trinity, three persons in one God, that the finished building may be for the worship of thy name, for the proclamation and the study of thy word and the better fitting of men's souls for thine everlasting kingdom,

PEOPLE: **In thy name we lay this cornerstone.**

MINISTER: Grant thy blessing upon us all here, and so strengthen the hands of thy servants that the building may be finished with joy and in beautiful completeness; and may every one of us be wholly dedicated to thy service, and our bodies be fit temples for the indwelling of the Holy Ghost.

We ask and offer all in the name of thy Son, our Savior, who hath taught us to pray, saying:

Our Father which art in heaven, Hallowed be thy name. Thy kingdom come. Thy will be done in earth, as it is in heaven. Give us this day our daily bread. And forgive us our debts, as we forgive our debtors. And lead us not into temptation, but deliver us from evil: For thine is the kingdom, and the power, and the glory, for ever. AMEN.

7. THE LAYING OF A CORNERSTONE OF AN EDUCATIONAL BUILDING [7]

MINISTER: Brethren, by the grace of God, we are permitted this day to begin the erection of an educational and youth building at this place. We do so, acknowledging that the many offerings already brought for this work have come from the generous hand of God.

PEOPLE: "The earth is the Lord's, and the fulness thereof; the world, and they that dwell therein."

MINISTER: This work has been planned for many years by the people of ——————— congregation.

PEOPLE: "They said, 'Let us rise up and build.' "

MINISTER: With faith, with prayer, and with sacrifice, we have now undertaken to build and equip this structure that the Christian faith of the present and future generations may be strong to labor for our God.

PEOPLE: "Let thy work appear unto thy servants, and thy glory unto their children. . . . And establish the work of our hands upon us; yea, the work of our hands establish thou it."

[7] As used in Saint Paul's Lutheran Church, New Orleans, Louisiana; William H. Wedig, minister.

SENTENCES USED BY VARIOUS CHURCH OFFICIALS
AS THEY BREAK THE SOD

"I now break this ground in the name of the Father, the Son and the Holy Ghost."

"Other foundation can no man lay than that is laid, which is Jesus Christ."

"The fear of the Lord is the beginning of wisdom: a good understanding have all they that do his commandments."

"Blessed is the nation whose God is the Lord; and the people whom he hath chosen for his own inheritance."

"Suffer little children, and forbid them not, to come unto me: for of such is the kingdom of God."

"Lord, I have loved the habitation of thy house, and the place where thine honour dwelleth."

RESPONSIVE PRAYER

MINISTER: O Lord, our God, we begin this work, in Jesus' name, for the strengthening of his kingdom on earth.

PEOPLE: **That we may grow in faith and knowledge of our Savior Jesus Christ.**

MINISTER: That still other generations may rise up which shall bless thy holy name.

PEOPLE: **That little children may learn the stories of Jesus and that older people may be kept on the pathway to heaven.**

MINISTER: That Christian education may be promoted and our moral conscience alerted to all evil.

PEOPLE: That childhood may be guided and youth may be challenged.

MINISTER: That Christian fellowship may be furthered, and that from thee we may better learn to love one another.

PEOPLE: That the kingdom of God may come to us, and that all men may be saved through our Lord Jesus Christ, to whom we give all praise and glory, world without end. AMEN.

8. MEDLEY OF SCRIPTURE VERSES FOR A BUILDING DEDICATION SERVICE [8]

(With minor alterations [9])

Thus says the Lord, Heaven is my throne and the earth is my footstool. What is this house which you would build for me, this place for my *abode?* . . . Unless the Lord builds the house those who build it labor in vain . . . The man to whom I will look is he who is humble and contrite of heart, who *hearkens* to my word.	Isa. 66:1
	Ps. 127:1
	Isa. 66:2*b*
In the four hundred and eightieth year after the people of Israel came out of the land of Egypt, in the fourth year	I Kings 6:1

---

[8] By Edward E. Chipman, minister, Sunset Hills Baptist Church, Omaha, Nebraska.

[9] Words in italics are alterations or additions.

of Solomon's reign . . . the word of the   I Kings 6:11, 14
Lord came to *him*, *saying*, "Concerning
this house which you are building, if
you will walk in my statutes and obey
my ordinances and keep my commandments and walk in them, then I will establish my word with you . . . and will
not forsake my people Israel."

So Solomon built the house and
finished it . . . Then *he* assembled the   I Kings 8:1a
elders of Israel, the heads and leaders
of the people . . . *and* stood before the   I Kings 8:22-24
altar of the Lord in the presence of all
the *people assembled*, and spread forth
his hands toward the heavens, and said,
"O Lord God . . . there is no God like
thee, in heaven above or on earth be-
neath. *Thou keepest* covenant and show-
est steadfast love to thy servants who
walk before thee with all their heart
. . . ; yea, thou didst speak with thy
mouth, and with thy hand hast fulfilled
thy promise . . . But will God indeed   I Kings 8:27-30
dwell on the earth? Behold heaven and
the highest heaven cannot contain thee.
How much less this house which *we*
have built! Yet have regard to the prayer
of thy servants and to their supplica-
tions . . . which *they* pray before thee
this day; that thy eyes may be open

night and day toward this house, the place of which thou hast said, 'My name shall be there! . . . And hearken to the supplication of thy people when they pray toward this place; yea, hear thou in heaven and when thou hearest, forgive.

. . . If a man sins against his neighbor; — I Kings 8:31a
. . . when thy people are defeated be- — I Kings 8:33a
cause they have sinned against thee;
. . . when heaven is shut up and there
is no rain; . . . if there is famine in the — I Kings 8:35
land, or pestilence or mildew or locust — I Kings 8:37-41
or caterpillar; *if the* enemy besieges or
whatever plague or sickness there is,
then whatever prayer, whatever supplication is made by any man or by all thy
people, each knowing the affliction of his
own heart and stretching out his hands
toward this house, then thou in heaven
thy dwelling place, and forgive, and act,
and render to each whose heart thou
knowest, according to all his ways (for
thou, thou only knowest the hearts of
the children of men): that they may
reverence thee all the days that they
may live.

. . . Likewise when a foreigner who is
not of *this* people comes and prays to- — I Kings 8:46
ward this house; . . . or if *thy people*

sin against thee,—for there is no man
who does not sin—yet if they lay it to
heart . . . and repent, with all their mind
and with all their heart and make supplication, then hear thou in heaven   I Kings 8:49
their prayer and supplication, and maintain their cause and forgive thy people
who have sinned against thee . . . Let   I Kings 8:52
thy eyes be open to the supplication of
thy servants, giving ear to them whenever they call upon thee.

. . . So may the Lord our God main   I Kings 8:59
tain the cause of his people as each day
requires, that all the peoples of the earth
may know the Lord is God; there is no
other. Let therefore our hearts be wholly   I Kings 8:61
true to the Lord our God, walking in
his statutes and keeping his commandments, as at this day.

So then you are no longer strangers   Eph. 2:19
and sojourners, but fellow citizens with
the saints, members of the household
of God. . . . You are built upon the foundation of the apostles and prophets, the
chief cornerstone being Jesus Christ, in
whom the whole structure is joined together and grows into a holy temple in
the Lord—in whom you also are built
. . . for a dwelling place of God in the
Spirit.

9. THE DEDICATION OF A CHURCH BUILDING [10]

The doors of the church shall be closed at the appointed hour of dedication. The officiating ministers shall proceed to the main door of the church on the outside and, knocking at the door, the minister shall say:

Open to me the gates of righteousness: I will go into them, and I will praise the Lord.

The door shall then be opened from within by the architect. The building contractor shall deliver the keys of the church to the chairman of the building committee. The chairman of the building committee shall deliver the keys to the president of the board of trustees, saying:

We deliver to you the keys of this building, erected for _____ Church.

The president of the board of trustees, receiving the keys, shall deliver them to the minister, saying:

In token that this building has been erected for _____ Church, on instructions given by the congregation, I deliver to you the keys thereof and pray you now to proceed to the service of dedication.

The minister then accepts the keys saying:

In the name of the officers and congregation, and for _____ Church, we accept the keys of this church in token of the trust committed to us, in the service of our Lord and Savior Jesus Christ. We are ready to proceed to the dedication.

Passing within the inner door of the church, the minister shall pause and say:

[10] As used in Grace Presbyterian Church, Jenkintown, Pennsylvania; Cecil Harding Jones, minister.

34

Peace be unto this house, and all who worship therein. Peace be to those that enter, and to those that go out therefrom. Peace be to those that love it, and to those that love the name of Jesus Christ our Lord.

THE ACT OF DEDICATION

MINISTER: Dearly beloved brethren: Forasmuch as it pleased Almighty God to put it into the heart of his servants to build this house for his worship, let us now fulfill the godly purpose for which we are assembled of dedicating it to the honor of God's most holy name. To the glory of God the Father, who has called us by his grace; To the honor of his Son, who loved us and gave himself for us; To the praise of the Holy Spirit, who illumines and sanctifies us;

PEOPLE: We dedicate this house.

MINISTER: For the worship of God in praise and prayer,
For the preaching of the everlasting gospel,
For the celebration of the holy sacraments,

PEOPLE: We dedicate this house.

MINISTER: For the comfort of all who mourn,
For strength of those who are tempted,
For light to those who seek the way,

PEOPLE: We dedicate this house.

MINISTER: For the hallowing of family life,
For teaching and guiding the young,
For the perfecting of the saints,

PEOPLE: We dedicate this house.

MINISTER: For the conversion of sinners,

For the promotion of righteousness,
For the extension of the kingdom of God,
PEOPLE: We dedicate this house.

MINISTER: In loving memory of those who have gone from us, whose hearts and hands have served in this church; With gratitude for all whose faith and consecrated gifts make this house possible; In gratitude for the labors of all those who love and serve this church and with prayers for all who shall worship in this house in years to come,

PEOPLE: We dedicate this house.

MINISTER: And now, as a people within the household of God, in the unity of faith, in the communion of saints, in love and good will to all, in gratitude for the gift of this house to be an habitation of God through the Spirit,

PEOPLE: We dedicate ourselves to Christ, to the worship of God, and the service of his kingdom, for the ministry of the open Bible, in the name of the Father, and of the Son, and of the Holy Spirit. AMEN.

PRAYER OF DEDICATION

DECLARATION OF DEDICATION

In the name of the Father, and of the Son, and of the Holy Spirit, I now declare this house to be forever set apart from all profane and common usages, and consecrated to the worship and service of almighty God; to whom be glory and majesty, dominion and power, for ever and ever. AMEN.

10. THE DEDICATION OF A HOUSE
OF WORSHIP [11]

THE SCRIPTURE: Ps. 84

MINISTER: How amiable are thy tabernacles, O Lord of hosts!

PEOPLE: My soul longeth, yea, even fainteth for the courts of the Lord:

MINISTER: My heart and my flesh crieth out for the living God.

PEOPLE: Yea, the sparrow hath found an house, and the swallow a nest for herself, where she may lay her young,

MINISTER: Even thine altars, O Lord of hosts, my King, and my God.

PEOPLE: Blessed are they that dwell in thy house: they will be still praising thee. Selah.

MINISTER: Blessed is the man whose strength is in thee; in whose heart are the ways of them.

PEOPLE: Who passing through the valley of Baca make it a well;

MINISTER: The rain also filleth the pools.

PEOPLE: They go from strength to strength, every one of them in Zion appeareth before God.

MINISTER: O Lord God of hosts, hear my prayer: give ear, O God of Jacob. Selah.

PEOPLE: Behold, O God our shield, and look upon the face of thine anointed.

[11] As used in the Lakeview Christian Church, Dallas, Texas; Kenneth H. Hay, minister.

MINISTER: For a day in thy courts is better than a thousand.

PEOPLE: **I had rather be a doorkeeper in the house of my God, than to dwell in the tents of wickedness.**

MINISTER: For the Lord God is a sun and a shield: the Lord will give grace and glory: no good thing will he withhold from them that walk uprightly.

PEOPLE: **O Lord of hosts, blessed is the man that trusteth in thee.**

THE LITANY OF DEDICATION

MINISTER: Having been blessed by our heavenly Father, through whose goodness we have come to this high hour, we now stand in his presence and to the glory and the service of his Son.

PEOPLE: **We dedicate this sanctuary.**

MINISTER: For the ministry of his word, for worship, prayer, and praise,

PEOPLE: **We dedicate this sanctuary.**

MINISTER: For comfort to those who mourn, for strength to those who are tempted, for grace to those who are afflicted, for every help to right living, for the salvation of men,

PEOPLE: **We dedicate this sanctuary.**

MINISTER: For the guidance of childhood, for the sanctity of the family, for the sacred unity of the home, for the purity of social life, for the teaching of temperance and chastity,

PEOPLE: **We dedicate this sanctuary.**

MINISTER: For the training of a good conscience, the teaching of a pure faith, the preaching of the gospel of Jesus Christ, the cultivation of the missionary spirit and the spread of the truth, as it is in him, to the uttermost parts of the earth,

PEOPLE: We dedicate this sanctuary.

MINISTER: For the education of body and mind and soul; for the fostering of truest patriotism, the best citizenship, the highest ideals, the noblest character; for the defense of all righteousness and unceasing war against all wickedness, in public and private life,

PEOPLE: We dedicate this sanctuary.

MINISTER: For the help of the poor, the relief of the needy, the instruction of the ignorant; for the consolation of the troubled; for peace to the distressed; for rest to the weary and heavy laden; for hope for the discouraged and disappointed; for the protection of the orphan, the widow, and the friendless; for welcome to the stranger; for the promotion of the brotherhood of man, the fellowship of righteousness, and the bringing in of the kingdom of God, and the unity of all God's people,

PEOPLE: We, the people of ———— Church here and now, consecrating ourselves anew, dedicate this house to the glory of the Father, and the Son and the Holy Spirit.

11. THE REDEDICATION OF A SANCTUARY [12]

MINISTER: Approximately _____ years ago the members and friends of this congregation erected and dedicated this building in which we now worship. Throughout these years it has served to the glory of God, and in the service of mankind, in ever-widening influence. During the past two or three years, under the guidance and direction of Almighty God our Heavenly Father, we have labored together and have come to this happy day and hour when we have redecorated (and/or recarpeted) his holy place, this sanctuary. This has come to pass through the co-operation of many persons within the membership of our congregation, who have given generously and sacrificially of time, effort, and money toward this goal. Much love, devotion, and sacrifice have gone into this project.

CHAIRMAN OF THE OFFICIAL BOARD: We commend all who have had a part in bringing this project to completion, and I present it to the minister for rededication.

MINISTER: To the glory of God, our Father; to the honor of Jesus Christ, our Lord and Savior; to the praise of the Holy Spirit, source of life and light,

PEOPLE: We rededicate this sanctuary.

MINISTER: For worship in prayer and song, for the ministry of the Word, for the celebration of the ordinances of Christ,

PEOPLE: We rededicate this sanctuary.

MINISTER: For the guidance of little children and youth

[12] As used in Quindaro Christian Church, Kansas City, Kansas; Russell M. Bythewood, minister.

into the Christian way of life, for instruction which is in righteousness,

PEOPLE: We rededicate this sanctuary.

MINISTER: For comfort of those who mourn, for strength to those who are tempted, for help in right living,

PEOPLE: We rededicate this sanctuary.

MINISTER: In grateful remembrance of those who have gone before us; in gratitude for the labors and sacrifices of our fathers and mothers in the faith; for the blessed hope of a house not made with hands, eternal in the heavens,

PEOPLE: We rededicate this sanctuary.

MINISTER: To the welfare of the living, to those whose ways are evil; to the strong souls that stoop to share the burden of their fellows; to the weak and defenseless; to the darkened mind, the tempted heart, the life weary and heavy-laden; and to all human needs,

PEOPLE: We rededicate this sanctuary.

MINISTER: To the proclamation of the Truth that sets man free, to the liberty of the children of God, to reverence for all worth of the past, and to the eager acceptance of all good which the future may unfold,

PEOPLE: We rededicate this sanctuary.

MINISTER: For the sanctification of the family, for the guidance of childhood, for the salvation of man,

PEOPLE: We rededicate this sanctuary.

MINISTER: For ennobling of honest toil, for quickening of

civic righteousness in our city, for promoting the consecration of all earthly powers to thy glory,

PEOPLE: We rededicate this sanctuary.

MINISTER: As a tribute of gratitude and love, an offering
of thanksgiving and praise, from those who have tasted
the cup of thy salvation and experienced the riches of
thy grace,

PEOPLE: We, the members and friends of this church, being compassed about with so great a cloud of witnesses, do here and now rededicate ourselves and this
sanctuary in the name of the Father, and of the Son,
and of the Holy Spirit. AMEN.

DEDICATION PRAYER (Minister)

12. THE DEDICATION OF AN
EDUCATIONAL BUILDING [13]

MINISTER: Having been prospered by the good hand of God
and enabled by his grace and power to erect this educational building to be used for the glory of his name,
we do now in his holy presence dedicate this building.

To the glory of God our Father, to the honor of
Jesus Christ, his Son and our Savior, to the praise of
the Holy Spirit, source of life and light,

PEOPLE: We dedicate this building.

[13] As used in the Lakewood Presbyterian Church, Lakewood, Ohio;
L. Wilson Kilgore, minister.

MINISTER: That the children and youth of today and of future generations may receive Christian education,

PEOPLE: We dedicate this building.

MINISTER: For the teaching and study of God's Holy Word, and for the Christian culture of all who may gather here,

PEOPLE: We dedicate this building.

MINISTER: For Christian fellowship and friendship and for the well being of the human body as the temple of the spirit of God.

PEOPLE: We dedicate this building.

MINISTER: That youth may come to know God as their heavenly Father and Jesus Christ as their personal Saviour and friend,

PEOPLE: We dedicate this building.

MINISTER: For the training of children in faith and character, for the summoning of youth to serviceable living, for the deepening of our sense of Christian brotherhood and for the furthering of the spirit of good will among all peoples,

PEOPLE: We dedicate this building.

MINISTER: For the missionary endeavor at home and abroad, for world-wide evangelism and education, till the kingdoms of this world become the kingdom of our Lord and of his Christ,

PEOPLE: We dedicate this building.

MINISTER: In loving memory of those who wrought here in days gone by, with sincere gratitude to those whose faith and gifts brought us to this joyful hour, and with supplication for all who shall worship here in years to come.

PEOPLE: We dedicate this building.

MINISTER AND PEOPLE: We, the people of this church and congregation, compassed about with a great cloud of witnesses, grateful for our heritage, sensible of the sacrifices of our fathers, do consecrate ourselves anew to worthy worship of God in this place. And to the continued service of God and man, we do now dedicate this educational building in the name of the Father and of the Son and of the Holy Ghost. AMEN.

13. LITANY FOR THE DEDICATION OF A CHURCH SPIRE [14]

MINISTER: Being prospered by the supporting hand of God to bring to completion in this spire the work we were called of him to accomplish,

PEOPLE: We dedicate this spire with gratitude and joy.

MINISTER: To inspire in every worshiper a sense of God who reigns in high purposes and pursuits, in transcendant power and love,

PEOPLE: We dedicate this spire, lifted and lifting to call our attention to divine ends and aims.

MINISTER: To call men's eyes and hearts to the spiritual

---

[14] As used in the First Congregational Church, Coloma, Michigan; Ralph W. Everroad, minister.

heights where the teachings and spirit of Christ beckon us to our highest aspirations,

PEOPLE: We dedicate this spire to indicate man's ability to rise above the levels of common humanity.

MINISTER: To call attention to the truth that the Holy Spirit came as a Comforter sent from on high to instill love and mercy and righteousness,

PEOPLE: We dedicate this spire in the hope that working with that Spirit we may attain the likeness of the Holy image which was the divine promise.

MINISTER: To call attention to the fact that the function of the Church is to lead upward toward the attainment of high ideals and lofty goals,

PEOPLE: We dedicate this spire with the fervent desire that the Church may ever point the way to peace and rectitude of life.

MINISTER: To focus the attention of all mankind on the urgency of the upward struggle toward eternal worth and to inspire in all a deep sense of the high calling whereunto we have been called,

PEOPLE: We dedicate this spire to the glory of God, the uplift of man, and the constant witness of the Church on earth to the gospel of Christ, for the service of whom it has been ordained.

ALL: And now unto that name which is above every name in heaven and on earth, we lift our hearts in adoration, and our words in praise, for unto him be the glory of the Church universal and eternal, through Jesus Christ our Lord.

14. THE DEDICATION OF A CHAPEL [15]

TRUSTEES: We present this chapel to be dedicated to the glory of God and the service of man.

MINISTER: By what name shall this chapel be known?

TRUSTEES: It shall be called ————————————.

ACT OF DEDICATION

MINISTER: To the glory of God the Father, who has called us by his grace; to the honor of his Son, who loved us and gave himself for us; to the praise of the Holy Spirit, who illumines and sanctifies us,

PEOPLE: We dedicate this chapel.

MINISTER: For the worship of God in prayer and praise, for the preaching of the everlasting gospel, for the celebration of the holy sacraments,

PEOPLE: We dedicate this chapel.

MINISTER: For the comfort of all who mourn, for strength to those who are tempted, for light to those who seek the way,

PEOPLE: We dedicate this chapel.

MINISTER: For the hallowing of family life, for teaching and guiding the young, for the perfecting of the saints,

PEOPLE: We dedicate this chapel.

MINISTER: For the conversion of sinners, for the promotion of righteousness, for the extension of the kingdom of God,

PEOPLE: We dedicate this chapel.

[15] As used in Michigan Street Methodist Church, Indianapolis, Indiana; R. M. Criswell, minister.

MINISTER: In the unity of a faith, in the bond of Christian brotherhood, in charity and good will to all,

PEOPLE: We dedicate this chapel.

MINISTER: In gratitude for the labors of all who love and serve this church, in loving memory of the faithful members of this church who have been called to their reward but hoped and prayed for the completion of the church in their day,

PEOPLE: We dedicate this chapel.

SANCTUS

PRAYER OF DEDICATION (unison)

We, the people of this church and congregation, compassed about with a great cloud of witnesses, grateful for our heritage, sensible of the sacrifice of our fathers in the faith, confessing that apart from us their work cannot be made perfect, do now dedicate ourselves anew to the worship and service of Almighty God; through Jesus Christ our Lord. AMEN.

PRAYER OF CONSECRATION (minister)

Grant, O Lord, that all who here share in the sacraments, the ministry of the Word, and the fellowship of praise may know that God is in this place, may hear thy voice within their hearts, and may go forth to extend to the uttermost bounds of life the Lord Christ's Kingdom. AMEN.

15. LITANY OF APPRECIATION FOR AN OLD CHURCH BUILDING [16]

MINISTER: Eternal Father, for this house which has served as our spiritual home for many years,

PEOPLE: We give thee our thanks.

MINISTER: In grateful remembrance of all those who helped prepare this house, that it might be fit for church use,

PEOPLE: We express our gratitude.

MINISTER: For wise and good leaders who planned the services and programs which took place within these walls,

PEOPLE: We give thee our thanks.

MINISTER: For the services of worship, including services of baptism and the Lord's Supper,

PEOPLE: We give thee our thanks.

MINISTER: For the joyous occasions of weddings, dinners, and special programs,

PEOPLE: We give thee our thanks.

MINISTER: For lessons taught here by faithful church-school teachers, both Sunday and weekday,

PEOPLE: We express our gratitude.

MINISTER: For all those people, influenced by the worship and fellowship in this house, who made decisions to follow Christ as their Savior,

PEOPLE: We express our gratitude.

MINISTER: For all the memories which this house holds for us in our growing awareness of thy presence,

PEOPLE: We give thee our thanks.

[16] Used in the Eastwood Baptist Church, Syracuse, New York; Nicholas Titus, minister.

PASTOR AND PEOPLE: And now, in grateful appreciation of the useful service of this house as our spiritual home, and to meet the challenge of growing needs for Christian education through more safe and modern facilities, we dedicate ourselves anew to the establishment of thy Kingdom. Through Jesus Christ, our Lord. AMEN.

16. A FAREWELL MESSAGE FROM THE MORTGAGE [17]

Dear Friends, for you this is a festive occasion. For _____ years you have looked forward to this day of my cremation, and now your aspirations are to be realized. In those _____ years it has been my lot to be a heavy burden to you. I have been looked upon as a drawback to the progress of this church. On very frequent occasions I have been the subject of much discussion in the meetings of the trustees, in the congregational meetings, and even in the very spiritual meetings of the session. You have planned and schemed to keep me from dying an unnatural death. Through the years I have been frowned upon and considered your worst enemy.

Frankly, your attitude has grieved me, for in reality I have been a good friend to you. I have even considered

[17] This may be used in connection with a service of mortgage burning. It was written by R. F. Egelhoff, an elder in the Second United Presbyterian Church of Buffalo, and was read just before the torch was applied to the mortgage.

myself a worthy worker in the church. Were it not for me this very building would not have been possible. Through these many years I have been the material incentive which urged you on to great and constant effort. Yes, I know that your great incentive has been a deeply founded spiritual one. However, it was I who gave you something tangible and conspicuously visible to work for. In so doing I held your interest, developed in you a united effort, and bolstered you spiritually.

If I have been of help and service to you, I am happy and am content now to submit to death and cremation. Before I go, however, may I leave a word of advice with you. As you carry on this great work of the church through the years ahead the incentive which I have furnished will not be with you. It is my firm belief, for the greatest results, a material incentive must be coupled with your spiritual incentive. Therefore, I urge upon you that you undertake the definite support of a specific work along Christian lines in fields other than your immediate church field. Preferably, this new work should be such that you may from year to year get a visible picture of its growth. Just as you strove unitedly to lay me in the ashes, so may you strive for the growth and success of this new undertaking.

Beware of sitting back complacently in the satisfaction of having accomplished your goal, for in complacency growth and progress die. May your experience with me be long remembered and may it have indelibly written on your memories the fact that the higher the goal the more earnest is the effort and the greater the joy of accomplishment.

Farewell, and may God guide you in the work ahead.

17. THE BURNING OF THE CHURCH MORTGAGE [18]

MINISTER: Blessed be the Lord God who doeth wondrous things.

PEOPLE: Blessed be his glorious name forever and ever. AMEN.

ALL: Being graciously prospered by the hand of our God in lifting the burden of debt from this church of Jesus Christ, we now, with joy in our hearts, are about to transform this cancelled mortgage, the symbol of our completed task, into the incense of prayer and thanksgiving.

MINISTER: In love for our church and in reverent memory of all those who by their services and sacrifices down through the years have bequeathed to us such valuable and beautiful property,

PEOPLE: We enter into this service.

MINISTER: With grateful appreciation of the generosity of members and friends, of the earnest and fruitful labors of organizations, and of the untiring services and prayers of the officers of this church,

PEOPLE: We gratefully share in this experience.

MINISTER: With a prayer that God shall continue to guide us with wisdom, bless us with a spirit of loyal unity, and inspire us to use our precious heritage to draw men unto himself,

[18] This service was devised for a congregation which desired a more informal responsive than is usually used. It was used in the First Baptist Church of Glenside-Wynote, Glenside, Pennsylvania. Maurice Eugene Levy was the pastor at the time of its use.

PEOPLE: We acknowledge that apart from him we can do nothing.

MINISTER: Dedicating ourselves anew to the work and support of this our beloved church, and through it to the extension of the kingdom of our Lord and Savior, Jesus Christ, throughout this our community, our nation, our world,

PEOPLE: We now burn this mortgage in the name of the Father, and of the Son, and of the Holy Spirit. **AMEN.**

(*While the photostat of the canceled mortgage burns the congregation rises to join in the Doxology.*)

18. THE DEDICATION OF A CHURCH PARLOR [19]

(*The following introductory statement may be read by the pastor or the president of the women's organization.*)

Good women, according to Scripture and personal observation, have contributed vastly to the spiritualizing of human relations and to the promotion of the Christian cause throughout the world. In matters pertaining to the kingdom of God "the matron and the maid" have much to their credit.

Ruth, Esther, Miriam, Mary, Anna, Elizabeth, Dorcas, and Lydia are scriptural heroines whose acquaintance en-

[19] As used in the Community Presbyterian Church, Parkdale, Oregon; James M. Brown, minister.

riches our lives. As this (name of room) fulfills the purpose of those who planned it these names with their hallowed origins will assume contemporary meaning as they come to signify the gracious, friendly, helpful fellowship of the women's groups of this church. Here new and greater traditions will be created as those enjoying its hospitality, study, work, pray, play, and plan together and form friendships as enduring as the mountaintop.

This room will also serve as a hallowed memorial, reminding the groups meeting here of the toils and triumphs of those who have shared in the work of the women's department. "To live in hearts we leave behind is not to die."

THE ACT OF DEDICATION

MINISTER: To the recognition of the service rendered by the women of the church in the promotion of all Christian interests,

PEOPLE: We dedicate this room.

MINISTER: To the creation of a homelike church, the building of a spiritual family of God in which women will find inspiration and guidance for more effective service,

PEOPLE: We dedicate this room.

MINISTER: To the moral strengthening of the community's life in every phase of its being, in the home, in the church, in the school, in business, and in all social relationships,

PEOPLE: We dedicate this room.

MINISTER: To the advancement of our part in the total program of the church, local and world-wide, that it may

more effectively and fruitfully sponsor and maintain
those causes which have to do with Christian education, philanthropy, temperance, economic justice, na-
tional probity and honor, and international good will,

PEOPLE: We dedicate this room.

MINISTER AND PEOPLE: Being prospered by the good hand
of God whose service is our joy, we have fitted and
furnished this room for the use of the women's de-
partments, naming it and now dedicating it in the
name of the Father, the Son, and the Holy Spirit.
AMEN.

PRAYER OF DEDICATION

II
FURNISHINGS AND EQUIPMENT

1. OFFICE FOR THE BLESSING
OF AN ALTAR [1]

MINISTER: In the name of the Father, and of the Son, and of the Holy Ghost,

PEOPLE: AMEN.

MINISTER: Our help is in the name of the Lord,

PEOPLE: Who made heaven and earth.

MINISTER: O Lord, open thou my lips,

PEOPLE: And my mouth shall show forth thy praise.

MINISTER: Make haste, O God, to deliver me,

PEOPLE: Make haste to help me, O Lord.

MINISTER: Glory be to the Father, and to the Son, and to the Holy Ghost,

PEOPLE: As it was in the beginning, is now, and ever shall be, world without end. AMEN.

MINISTER: O send out thy light and thy truth, let them lead me,

PEOPLE: Let them bring me unto thy holy hill, and to thy tabernacles.

MINISTER: Then will I go unto the altar of God,

PEOPLE: Unto God my exceeding joy.

MINISTER: The sacrifices of God are a broken spirit,

PEOPLE: A broken and a contrite heart, O God, thou wilt not despise.

MINISTER: The Lord be with you,

PEOPLE: And with thy spirit.

MINISTER: Lift up your hearts,

[1] Adapted from "Occasional Services," published by the United Lutheran Board of Publication. Used by permission.

PEOPLE: **We lift them up unto the Lord.**

MINISTER: Let us give thanks unto the Lord our God,

PEOPLE: **It is meet and right to do so.**

MINISTER: It is truly meet, right, and salutary, that we should at all times, and in all places, give thanks unto thee, O Lord, Holy Father, Almighty Everlasting God, who on the tree of the cross didst give salvation unto mankind through Christ our Lord; and we humbly beseech thee, let thy unspeakable loving kindness and tender mercy be with us, O God, in whose honor and for whose glory, we thine unworthy servants, invoking thy holy name, do dedicate this altar; graciously hearken unto our petitions and bless and hallow it; and grant that this, our offering, may be acceptable and pleasing unto thee who livest and reignest, one God, world without end.

Blest and dedicated be this altar to the honor and glory of God, in the name of the Father, and of the Son, and of the Holy Ghost. AMEN.

Blessing and honor, and glory, and power, be unto him that sitteth upon the throne; and unto the Lamb, for ever and ever. Alleluia. AMEN.

Let Us Pray

Almighty God, everlasting Father, who dost refresh us as we have need, and dost strengthen our faith with heavenly food, so that we go from strength to strength: Vouchsafe to all who receive at this altar the holy sacrament of the body and blood of thy dear Son, to approach this holy mystery with pure hearts, believing desire, and devout thanksgiving, that, comforted with

58

thy eternal love and goodness, they may be nourished and strengthened in faith, live in love and to the praise of thy holy name, and finally attain to thy presence in eternity; through the same Jesus Christ, thy Son, our Lord. AMEN.

O God, who dost call all men to thee, and who dost graciously receive all them that come: Vouchsafe thy pardon to all those who here confess their sins; bestow the comfort of thy spirit on those who humbly and faithfully bring thee their needs and sorrows; accept the praise and worship that are offered here; and grant that many may find thee in this place, and finding thee, be filled in soul and body with all things needful; and finally, with all thine own, be united in that communion with thee which is eternal in the heavens, where thou livest and reignest, ever One God, world without end. AMEN.

The blessing of Almighty God, the Father, the Son, and the Holy Ghost descend and rest upon this altar and abide in this holy place and with us all now and evermore. AMEN.

2. THE DEDICATION OF MEMORIALS [2]

MINISTER: For as much as there has been presented to this church in memory of _____

[2] This service was used in the Evangelical United Brethren Church, Warrensville, Pennsylvania. It was arranged by the minister, Carl V. Bretz. Memorials received included baptismal font, communion table, paraments, vases, candlesticks, and cross.

these memorials to be dedicated to the glory and praise of God, we do accept these gifts as a sacred trust and shall guard them reverently, in honor of the life (lives) in whose memory they are given. It is fitting and proper that we should thus remember our friends and honor our God.

PEOPLE: **Blessed be the name of the Lord, from this time forth and forevermore.**

MINISTER: It was Christ our Lord who instituted the sacrament of baptism and gave the command to teach all nations, baptizing them in the name of the Father and of the Son and of the Holy Ghost. It is for this purpose that we dedicate the baptismal font.

PEOPLE: **Bless the Lord, O my soul; and all that is within me, bless his holy name.**

MINISTER: The communion table is none other than the table of our Lord. It should bring to our minds—"eat"; "drink"; "this do in remembrance of me."

PEOPLE: **Bless the Lord, O my soul, and forget not all his benefits.**

MINISTER: The rich colors and symbolism of the paraments are constant reminders of great truths and doctrines and add beauty and dignity to the services of the church.

PEOPLE: **Let the beauty of the Lord our God be upon us.**

MINISTER: Vases are provided so that flowers may be placed on the communion table not as a matter of mere ornaments, but to the glory of God as an expression of devotion, and that the sanctuary may be beautified.

PEOPLE: O all ye green things upon the earth bless ye the Lord; praise him and magnify him forever.

MINISTER: Jesus is the true light which lighteth every man. As we see the candlesticks holding aloft the lighted candles, we are reminded that Jesus said, "I am the light of the world,"

PEOPLE: How excellent is thy loving kindness, O God! . . . For with thee is the fountain of life; in thy light shall we see light.

MINISTER: But God forbid that I should glory, save in the cross of our Lord Jesus Christ. "The cross to the earliest members of the church represented their master, who was all in all to them . . . to represent all the faith . . . the person of Christ, his death for man, and the life and death of man in Christ,"

PEOPLE: Blessing, and glory, and wisdom, and thanksgiving, and honor, and power, and might be unto our God forever, and ever. AMEN.

PRAYER

3. THE DEDICATION OF APPOINTMENTS AND MEMORIALS [3]

ORGAN PRELUDE

PROCESSIONAL HYMN: "Lead On, O King Eternal"

[3] As used by the Trinity Lutheran Church, Rockford, Illinois.

CONFESSION OF SINS

MINISTER: In the name of the Father, and of the Son and of the Holy Ghost. Amen. Beloved in the Lord! Let us draw near with a true heart, and confess our sins unto God our Father, beseeching Him, in the name of our Lord Jesus Christ, to grant us forgiveness. Our help is in the name of the Lord.

PEOPLE: **Who made heaven and earth.**

MINISTER: I said, I will confess my transgressions unto the Lord.

PEOPLE: **And thou forgavest the iniquity of my sin.**

MINISTER: Almighty God, our Maker and Redeemer, we poor sinners confess unto thee, that we are by nature sinful and unclean, and that we have sinned against thee by thought, word, and deed. Wherefore we flee for refuge to thine infinite mercy, seeking and imploring thy grace, for the sake of our Lord Jesus Christ.

PEOPLE: **O most merciful God, who has given thine only begotten son to die for us, have mercy upon us, and for his sake grant us remission of all our sins; and by thy Holy Spirit increase in us true knowledge of thee, and of thy will, and true obedience to thy word, to the end that by thy grace we may come to everlasting life, through Jesus Christ our Lord. AMEN.**

MINISTER: Almighty God, our Heavenly Father, hath had mercy upon us and hath given his only son to die for us, and for his sake forgiveth us all our sins. To them that believe on his name, he giveth power to become sons of God and bestoweth upon them his Holy Spirit.

He that believeth and is baptized, shall be saved. Grant this, O Lord, unto us all.

PEOPLE: AMEN.

SCRIPTURE: Josh. 24:22-28; Matt. 26:6-13.

THE SERVICE OF DEDICATION

MINISTER: How amiable are thy tabernacles, O Lord of hosts! My soul longeth, yea, even fainteth for the courts of the Lord:

PEOPLE: **My heart and my flesh crieth out for the living God.**

MINISTER: Yea, the sparrow hath found an house, and the swallow a nest for herself, where she may lay her young, even thine altars, O Lord of hosts, my King, and my God.

PEOPLE: **Blessed are they that dwell in thy house: they will be still praising thee. Selah.**

MINISTER: For a day in thy courts is better than a thousand.

PEOPLE: **I had rather be a doorkeeper in the house of my God, than to dwell in the tents of wickedness.**

MINISTER: For the Lord God is a sun and shield: the Lord will give grace and glory: no good thing will be withheld from them that walk uprightly.

PEOPLE: **O Lord of hosts, blessed is the man that trusteth in thee.**

MINISTER: Almighty God, our Heavenly Father, we thank thee for the appointments of thy holy sanctuary. This altar, symbol of thy presence, thy mercy seat, upon which we would bestow our gifts, and from thy mercy seat may thy people, confirmed and married receive thy blessing.

PEOPLE: To thee we dedicate this altar.

MINISTER: This pulpit erected that thy everlasting gospel may be proclaimed.

PEOPLE: To thee we dedicate this pulpit.

MINISTER: For the reading of thy eternal word, that thy people may be led by thy word.

PEOPLE: To thee we dedicate this lectern.

MINISTER: To fulfill the Lord's last command—"Go ye . . . and teach all nations, baptizing them in the name of the Father, and of the Son, and of the Holy Ghost,"

PEOPLE: To thee we dedicate this baptismal font.

MINISTER: These pews for the use of thy people, as they come to worship thee, to sing thy praises, and to hear thy word.

PEOPLE: To thee we dedicate these pews.

MINISTER: The tower bells to send out a call to worship, reminder of thy will to meet thy people.

PEOPLE: To thee we dedicate these tower bells.

MINISTER: All appointments of this _____ Church, the cross, the candle holders, the vessels set apart for holy purposes, and all furnishings, gifts and memorials,

PEOPLE: To thee we dedicate these gifts.

MINISTER: In the name of the Father, and of the Son, and of the Holy Ghost, I do now declare these furnishings, gifts, and memorials in this _____ Church to be forever set apart to the worship and services of our Lord and Saviour, to whom be glory and majesty, dominion and power, forever and ever. AMEN.

THE SERMON

THE HYMN: "Now Thank We All Our God," Kratzman

THE BENEDICTION: Sevenfold Amen: Silent Prayer

ORGAN POSTLUDE

4. THE DEDICATION OF A MEMORIAL BAPTISMAL FONT [4]

MINISTER: "Holy baptism witnesses and seals unto us the washing away of our sins through Jesus Christ. For we are baptized into the name of the Father, and of the Son, and of the Holy Spirit."

In the name of God, the Father, who seals unto us his covenant of Grace; in the name of the Son, by whom God assures us of our cleansing through the blood of Christ; in the name of the Holy Spirit, through whom God promises that he will dwell in us and sanctify us to be members of Christ,

PEOPLE: We dedicate this baptismal font.

MINISTER: For the baptism of children as heirs of the kingdom of God and his covenant; for the baptism of adults as a witness to their repentance, and to their faith in the Lord Jesus Christ,

[4] As used in the First Reformed Church, College Point, New York.

PEOPLE: We dedicate this baptismal font.

MINISTER: To the memory of_____, and in remembrance of his (her) devotion to God and the work and worship of his church on earth,

PEOPLE: We dedicate this baptismal font.

PRAYER (unison):

Father of our Lord Jesus Christ, of whom every family in heaven and on earth is named, bless all who come to this font to receive the symbol of thy forgiving love and redeeming power. May fathers and mothers be true to the vows here taken in thy presence. May the penitent go forth to live a life sanctified by our blessed Savior. Wash us from our iniquity and cleanse us from our sin. Restore unto us the joy of thy salvation; through Jesus Christ, our Lord. AMEN.

5. THE DEDICATION OF A BAPTISTERY POOL [5]

MINISTER: Jesus said, "All power is given unto me in heaven and in earth. Go ye therefore, and teach all nations, baptizing them in the name of the Father, and of the Son, and of the Holy Ghost: Teaching them to observe all things whatsoever I have commanded you: and, lo, I am with you alway, even unto the end of the world."

Saint Peter, on the day of Pentecost, called upon the

[5] William H. Leach.

people saying, "Repent, and be baptized every one of you in the name of Jesus Christ for the remission of sins, and ye shall receive the gift of the Holy Ghost."

We are proud to belong to the group known as baptizers and we seek through the dedication of this baptistery to renew our faith in the promise which our Lord has made to his people.

Will you, the people of this congregation, receive this baptistery pool which symbolizes the flowing water of the Jordan River in which John baptized Jesus?

PEOPLE: We do so receive this baptistery.

MINISTER: Do you reaffirm your faith that baptism in the name of Jesus Christ, in the spirit of repentance, brings the transmission of sins?

PEOPLE: We do so believe and declare.

MINISTER: Now that you are receiving in your church this new and beautiful pool, do you promise to keep in your hearts the promise which Jesus made, and teach it to your children that they may share in that promise?

PEOPLE: We so do promise.

MINISTER: Will you continually pray that your own baptism may be more than that of water; that you have assurance that you have been baptized not alone in the water but in the life of the Savior?

PEOPLE: We do so promise.

PRAYER OF DEDICATION

To thee O God, our heavenly father, we lift our voices and our hearts. May the heaven descending dove which was visible when Jesus was baptized by John be seen through our spiritual eyes, as the people come to this baptistery to affirm their Christian faith. We pray thee, our Father, that thou wilt receive and sanctify those who express their repentance in the symbol of baptism in this pool, and number them among thy faithful children.

6. THE DEDICATION OF CHANCEL FURNITURE [6]

MINISTER: To proclaim the good news of Jesus Christ, to feed with spiritual food those who worship here, to herald peace on earth to men of good will, to declare God's eternal laws of justice, mercy and humility,

PEOPLE: We dedicate this pulpit.

MINISTER: To the reading of the Holy Scripture, the word of God for our inspiration, doctrine, reproof, and instruction in righteousness,

PEOPLE: We dedicate this lectern.

MINISTER: To proclaim the whole counsel of God, a light unto the path of every day,

PEOPLE: We dedicate this Holy Bible.

MINISTER: For the skillful craftsmanship of thy servants who have created the chapel lights we praise thee and to illuminate those who worship here,

PEOPLE: We dedicate these lights and chapel lanterns.

[6] As used in Annie Laurie Warren Chapel of the Peachtree Christian Church, Atlanta, Georgia; Robert W. Burns, minister.

MINISTER: To begin in seeking God's favor for each Christian home which is here started,

PEOPLE: We dedicate this prayer bench.

MINISTER: To provide a place of dignity and comfort for those who worship here,

PEOPLE: We dedicate these pews and chairs.

7. THE DEDICATION OF MEMORIAL COMMUNION WARE [7]

MINISTER: That the ordinance of the Lord's Supper may be observed with appropriate beauty and dignity,

PEOPLE: We dedicate this communion ware.

MINISTER: That whenever we see the bread on these plates we may recall our Lord who said, "I am the bread of life,"

PEOPLE: We dedicate these communion plates.

MINISTER: That as we take bread from these plates we may be reminded of the body of our Lord which was broken for our sakes,

PEOPLE: We dedicate these communion plates.

MINISTER: That whenever we see these communion trays and receive from them our cup, we may be reminded of the blood of our Lord which was poured out on our behalf,

PEOPLE: We dedicate these communion trays.

[7] As used in First Baptist Church, Wildwood, New Jersey; J. Francis Peak, minister.

MINISTER: That when we see the cross on the cover of these trays we may recall the sacrifice of our Lord and consider that from his cross we may draw strength to help us in time of need to bear our own burdens;

PEOPLE: We dedicate these communion trays.

MINISTER: That memory of _____, whose name appears on the communion tray covers, may be perpetuated by the use of these beautiful articles,

PEOPLE: We dedicate this communion ware.

PRAYER (*unison*)

Our Father in heaven, we thank thee for this simple memorial act by which we remember our Lord Jesus Christ, and in remembering him also remember the one who served this church so long and faithfully. We thank thee for the concern of the deacons and deaconesses who prepare our service with care and dignity. We offer to thee our new communion ware, and with it we would dedicate ourselves to a sincere seeking of thy Spirit, through the observance of our Lord's Supper. Through Jesus Christ our Lord. AMEN.

8. THE DEDICATION OF CROSS AND CANDLESTICKS [8]

MINISTER: We come to this moment in our worship when we pause to meditate upon the thoughtfulness of

[8] As used by the Overland Christian Church, Overland, Missouri.

others, whose love for their dearly departed ones will be kept fresh by a living memorial to them. Their generosity to us makes possible a more beautiful house of worship. It will make the experience of worship more meaningful to us all, and will serve as a constant reminder that our faith is best carried on when we serve in the spirit of the cross, undergirded by our prayers that rise continually before God as the cloud of smoke that ascends from the candlestick.

We are most grateful for those who have made these living memorials possible.

That we may be reminded of him who said, "If any man will come after me, let him deny himself, and take up his cross, and follow me,"

PEOPLE: We dedicate this cross.

MINISTER: That we may exemplify the spirit of the one who spoke, "God forbid that I should glory, save in the cross of our Lord Jesus Christ,"

PEOPLE: We dedicate this cross.

MINISTER: And that we may live our Christian faith according to the words of Jesus, "who for the joy that was set before him endured the cross, despising the shame, and is set down at the right hand of the throne of God,"

PEOPLE: We dedicate this cross.

MINISTER: In the spirit of our Lord who said, "men light a candle, and put it . . . on a candlestick; and it giveth light unto all that are in the house," and "let your light

71

so shine before men, that they may see your good works, and glorify your Father which is in heaven,"

PEOPLE: We dedicate these candlesticks.

MINISTER: That we might be reminded that the church must give forth its light, and that judgment comes to the church which does not have its lamps burning by having its candlestick removed,

PEOPLE: We dedicate these candlesticks.

ALL: As the continual burning of the lamp was symbolic of the continuing prosperity of the individual or the family, so may the burning of these candles call us to the continuing prosperity of all that wait before God.

DEDICATORY PRAYER

DEDICATORY HYMN: "In the cross of Christ I glory"

9. THE DEDICATION OF MEMORIAL LIGHTS [9]

MINISTER: The people that walked in darkness have seen a great light: they that dwell in the land of the shadow of death, upon them hath the light shined.

PEOPLE: Then Jesus spake unto them saying, "I am the light of the world: he that followeth me shall not walk in darkness, but shall have the light of life."

MINISTER: For God, who commanded the light to shine out of darkness, hath shined in our hearts, to give the

[9] As used in the United Presbyterian Church, Mumford, New York; Donald C. Macleod, minister.

72

light of the knowledge of the glory of God in the face of Jesus Christ.

PEOPLE: Let your light so shine before men, that they may see your good works, and glorify your Father which is in heaven.

MINISTER: To the glory of God, creator of the universe, who in the beginning said, "Let there be light," and there was light,

PEOPLE: We dedicate these lights.

MINISTER: To the glory of Jesus Christ, who came as light to the world, that whosoever believeth in him, should not abide in darkness,

PEOPLE: We dedicate these lights.

MINISTER: To the glory of the Holy Spirit, by whom, in all ages, the minds of men have been illumined,

PEOPLE: We dedicate these lights.

MINISTER: In honor of those, who in the night of darkness, lighted the lamp of truth, by which succeeding generations were led to liberty and light,

PEOPLE: We dedicate these lights.

MINISTER: In honor of those who zealously guarded that light throughout the centuries, protecting it against those who loved darkness rather than light,

PEOPLE: We dedicate these lights.

MINISTER: In loving memory of those whom we have known and loved, who here found a spiritual sanctuary, and in their lifetime helped maintain that light that has served as a lamp unto our feet and a light unto our path,

PEOPLE: We dedicate these lights.

MINISTER: To the glory of God, and in deep appreciation of the love behind the gift, we now accept these memorial lights in loving memory of _____.

MINISTER AND PEOPLE: The Lord bless us and keep us. The Lord make his face to shine upon us and be gracious unto us. The Lord lift up the light of his countenance upon us and give us peace. AMEN.

10. THE DEDICATION OF A CROSS [10]

MINISTER: In a world where there is so much evil among men in whose hearts there is so much sin, the cross of Christ stands as an everlasting sign of God's suffering love and plan of redemption. No other symbol of the Christian religion has the significance and meaning to Christians and none other is so precious as the cross.

In the name of the Father and of the Son and of the Holy Spirit,

PEOPLE: We dedicate this cross.

MINISTER: To the glory of God, who so loved the world that he gave his only begotten Son, that whosoever believeth in him should not perish, but have everlasting life,

PEOPLE: We dedicate this cross.

[10] As used in the Gunton Temple Memorial Presbyterian Church, Washington, D. C.; Eric Lindsay Cowall, minister.

MINISTER: "They took Jesus, and led him away. And he, bearing his cross went forth, into a place called the place of a skull . . . where they crucified him."

PEOPLE: **In memory of the death of Jesus Christ upon the cross, we dedicate this cross.**

MINISTER: "Then said Jesus unto his disciples, 'If any man will come after me, let him deny himself, take up his cross, and follow me.' "

PEOPLE: **In memory of the cross Jesus bids us bear, we dedicate this cross.**

MINISTER: "Father, forgive them; for they know not what they do."

PEOPLE: **In memory of the cross of forgiveness whereon God forgives mankind its sins, we dedicate this cross.**

MINISTER: To the eternal honor of Christ, the Lord who, upon the cross gave himself a willing sacrifice for the sins of the whole world,

PEOPLE: **We dedicate this cross.**

MINISTER: To the perpetual reminding of the Church that the cross is its changeless symbol of salvation and the source of its power to triumph,

PEOPLE: **We dedicate this cross.**

MINISTER: To the abiding memory of the devoted Christian men and women for whom this memorial is given, to whose love for Christ, and service in his Church, this cross shall serve as a constant reminder,

PEOPLE: **We dedicate this cross.**

MINISTER: To the devoted faithfulness of those who in this

latest hour through their gifts and consecrated service have made this memorial possible,

PEOPLE: We dedicate this cross.

MINISTER: To the increasing triumph of Christ and his church, through the redeeming love of God, and to the ultimate acceptance of the cross as the way of life for men and nations,

PEOPLE: We dedicate this cross.

MINISTER: That the cross, within the quietness and beauty of God's house, may be a silent teacher, speaking the power and peace of the Savior to troubled minds and hearts,

PEOPLE: We dedicate this cross.

MINISTER: That the radiance of the cross, falling upon God's people worshiping in his presence, may dispel all darkness of sin, doubt, and fear and may shed within their hearts the light of divine forgiveness,

PEOPLE: We dedicate this cross.

MINISTER: That the abiding presence of the cross in the sanctuary may be a constant challenge to all who behold it to enthrone in their lives the Christ, who has given the cross its glory, and to accept his way of unselfish love as the rule of life,

PEOPLE: We dedicate this cross.

HYMN:

When I survey the wondrous cross
On which the Prince of Glory died,

My richest gain I count but loss,
  And pour contempt on all my pride.

PRAYER OF DEDICATION

O God, most merciful and gracious, bless to thine own service and to the spiritual enrichment of all thy people who shall gather in this place, this cross, which we have dedicated to thee, and to the ministry of this church. In the quietness and beauty of this, thy house, may its unspoken but searching message bring guidance to the perplexed, strength to the burdened, faith to the faltering, comfort to the sorrowing, conviction to the sinner, and forgiveness to the penitent. Through its radiance, symbolic of the mission of our Lord Jesus Christ, the light of the world, may we be led into closer friendship with the Christ, who said, "And I, if I be lifted up, will draw all men unto me." Through Jesus Christ our Lord. AMEN.

11. THE DEDICATION OF MEMORIAL ALTAR VASES [11]

(*The following introductory statement may be read by the pastor, the chairman of the board, or some designated member of the congregation.*)

It is our pleasure this morning to accept and dedicate the altar vases presented in memory of _____.

[11] As used in the First Congregational Church, Coloma, Michigan; Ralph W. Everroad, minister.

Speaking for this congregation, I accept this beautiful memorial gift, with our sincere appreciation and the assurance that not only will it help to perpetuate the memory of our long time friend and faithful member, but it will add beauty and dignity to our chancel and altar, and add grace to the worship we offer to God and to his Son, our Lord.

May I invite all present to participate in the consecration of this memorial?

THE SERVICE OF ACCEPTANCE AND DEDICATION

MINISTER: With gratitude to one who, through many years has given himself (herself) with unfailing devotion to this church of which we are a part,

PEOPLE: We accept this gift.

MINISTER: To the glory of God who filled the earth with grace and fragrance, and has brightened the land with the fairness of flowers,

PEOPLE: We dedicate this gift.

MINISTER: With devotion to our Lord Jesus Christ who considered the meaning of the lilies, and found in the humblest flowers the holiest messages,

PEOPLE: We dedicate this gift.

MINISTER: To call attention to the quiet uplift and comfort of the Holy Spirit, seeking to implant more of the beauty of holiness in the hearts of men,

PEOPLE: We dedicate these vases.

MINISTER: To the hope that our prayers may be helped to ascend like garlands of beauty, and our worship be made fragrant with true devotion and consecration,

PEOPLE: We dedicate this gift.

PRAYER OF DEDICATION:

Almighty God, who hast given, and dost restore to us those whom we delight to hold in memory, and who having created the great temple of all life, endowing it with endless beauties of nature, and lackest nothing, yet desirest our worship in the sanctuary, accept we beseech thee, the offering of these vases and these flowers, consecrating them by thy power and blessing to holy use; and may all who worship here in these days and in the days to come, find inspiration therein, and be lifted up toward thee, the source and summit of all being and beauty. We ask in the name of Jesus Christ our Lord. AMEN.

12. THE DEDICATION OF A PULPIT BIBLE [12]

MINISTER: In grateful remembrance of all who have lived unselfishly, who have loved their neighbors more than themselves, who have loved their country more than their own private ends,

PEOPLE: We dedicate this pulpit Bible.

MINISTER: In special remembrance of our departed brother (sister), _____, who gave the last full measure of service in loving devotion to his (her) country, his (her) neighbors, and his (her) God,

PEOPLE: We dedicate this pulpit Bible.

[12] As used in the First Baptist Church, East Chicago, Indiana; Theodore N. Johnson, minister.

MINISTER: For our frequent neglect of God's holy word, for our many failures to heed its precepts, and to obey its commandments,

PEOPLE: We ask thy pardon, O God.

MINISTER: In solemn dedication to the captain of our salvation, Christ Jesus, in prayerful reaffirmation of our vows of allegiance to God and country, in hopeful reconsecration to the ideals of the kingdom of God,

PEOPLE: We ask for thy blessing upon this book and this pulpit, O God. AMEN.

READING OF THE FIRST SCRIPTURE LESSON: Eph. 6:10-20

13. THE DEDICATION OF OFFERING PLATES [13]

MINISTER: In the name of the Father, the Son, and the Holy Spirit,

PEOPLE: We dedicate these offering plates.

MINISTER: As vessels through which the tithes and offerings of the people might be presented unto the Lord in gratitude and praise,

PEOPLE: We dedicate these offering plates.

MINISTER: As symbols of sacrifice and divine love,

PEOPLE: We dedicate these offering plates.

MINISTER: As expressions of beauty and endurance,

[13] As used in Trinity Evangelical United Brethren Church, Mifflin, Pennsylvania; C. L. Leber, minister.

PEOPLE: We dedicate these offering plates.

MINISTER: As altar pieces that silently challenge us to the faithful exercise of stewardship of substance, time, and energy,

PEOPLE: We dedicate these offering plates.

MINISTER: As tokens of our desire to see God's kingdom come and his will done upon the earth, even as in heaven,

PEOPLE: We dedicate these offering plates and ourselves to thee and thy service, O Lord. AMEN.

14. BIBLICAL VERSES FOR THE DEDICATION OF AN ORGAN [14]

MINISTER: Jubal . . . was the father of all such as handle the harp and organ. (Gen. 4:21.)

PEOPLE: They take the timbrel and harp, and rejoice at the sound of the organ. (Job 21:12.)

MINISTER: Honor and majesty are before him: strength and beauty are in his sanctuary. (Ps. 96:6.)

PEOPLE: O worship the Lord in the beauty of holiness. (Ps. 96:9.)

MINISTER: Praise ye the Lord. Sing unto the Lord a new song and his praise in the congregation of the saints. (Ps. 149:1.)

PEOPLE: Praise him with stringed instruments and organs. (Ps. 150:4.)

[14] Arranged by James C. Perkins.

MINISTER: Make a joyful noise unto the Lord, all ye lands. (Ps. 100:1.)

PEOPLE: Speaking to yourselves in psalms and hymns and spiritual songs, singing and making melody in your hearts to the Lord. (Eph. 5:19.)

MINISTER: I will sing with the spirit, and I will sing with the understanding also. (I Cor. 14:15.)

PEOPLE: And I heard the voice of harpers harping with their harps. (Rev. 14:2.)

MINISTER: And they sung as it were a new song before the throne. (Rev. 14:3.)

MINISTER AND PEOPLE: And they sing the song of Moses, the servant of God, and the song of the Lamb, saying, Great and marvelous are thy works, Lord God Almighty; just and true are thy ways, thou King of saints . . . for thou only art holy: for all nations shall come and worship before thee. (Rev. 15:3, 4.)

15. THE DEDICATION OF AN ORGAN—I [15]

MINISTER: That the ministry of music in this church may be to the glory of God, let us dedicate this organ.

PEOPLE: To the glory of God, the Father Almighty, that we may more worthily worship him, we dedicate this organ.

[15] As arranged by Edward E. Chipman and used in the Chaffee Community Baptist Church, Denver, Colorado.

MINISTER: To the praise of Jesus Christ, the saviour of mankind, at whose birth the angels sang, that our joy in him may find more worthy expression, we dedicate this organ.

PEOPLE: **And to the holy spirit, in whose fellowship the discords of life are lost in the glorious harmony of God, we dedicate this organ.**

MINISTER: To the church of Jesus Christ and its mission in the world; the comforting of the sorrowful, the strengthening of the weak, the cheering of the weary, the curing of sin-sick souls, the swelling of the chorus of praise, we dedicate this organ.

PEOPLE: **To the cause of greater religious fervor, and a deeper appreciation of the sacred hymns that are ours, the profound expressions of God-inspired souls, we dedicate this organ.**

MINISTER AND PEOPLE: Here in thy holy presence, O God, surrounded by so great a cloud of witnesses of all the ages, grateful for our lofty inheritance, and conscious of the sacrifices of those who have gone before, we do now dedicate ourselves and this organ to thy service, and to the service of mankind, in the name and spirit of Jesus Christ our Lord.

HYMNAL PRAYER: Tune, "All Saints, New" (*People standing, all singing.*)

Great God, to Thee we consecrate
  Our voices and our skill;
We bid the pealing organ wait
  To speak alone Thy will.

Lord, while the music round us floats,
  May earthborn passions die;
O grant its rich and swelling notes
  May lift our souls on high!

                          AMEN

16. THE DEDICATION OF AN ORGAN—II [16]

MINISTER: Beloved in Christ, forasmuch as God has put into our hearts the desire to dedicate this instrument of music as an aid to our worship of him in this holy place, it is right that we should now rededicate it to him and set it apart to the holy use for which it was designed. To the glory of God, author of all goodness and beauty, giver of all skill of mind and hand,

PEOPLE: We dedicate this organ.

MINISTER: In the faith of our Lord Jesus Christ, who has inspired men to offer in his praise their best in music and song,

PEOPLE: We dedicate this organ.

MINISTER: Moved by the Holy Spirit, our guide in the worship of God and our helper in the understanding of truth and beauty,

PEOPLE: We dedicate this organ.

MINISTER: To kindle the flame of devotion, that the people of God who here assemble may worship the Father in spirit and in truth,

[16] As used in the West Side Presbyterian Church, Ridgewood, New Jersey; Arthur Morris Hughes, minister.

84

PEOPLE: We dedicate this organ.

MINISTER: To bear up the melody of psalm and hymn and spiritual song in such wise that men may go forth from this house of God with high resolve to do his holy will,

PEOPLE: We dedicate this organ.

MINISTER: To comfort the sorrowful and cheer the faint, to bring purity and peace into human hearts, and to lead all who hear it in the way of eternal life,

PEOPLE: We dedicate this organ.

PRAYER OF DEDICATION (unison)

Heavenly Father, we give unto thee the utmost we can render of power and riches, and might and honor, and glory and blessing. We thank thee that thou hast so made us that by music our hearts can be lifted up to thee. As thou hast called us to thy service in this church, grant that we may so love thee that thy glory may fill this house. Send thy spirit upon us that we may sing with the spirit and with the understanding also, and that we may become partakers of the inheritance of the saints in light, who sing the new song about thy throne. Through Jesus Christ our Lord. AMEN.

ASCRIPTION OF PRAISE:

Holy, Holy, Holy! Lord God Almighty!
Early in the morning our song shall rise to Thee;
Holy, Holy, Holy! merciful and mighty!
God in Three Persons, blessed Trinity.

17. THE DEDICATION OF ORGAN AND TOWER CHIMES [17]

MINISTER: That the ministry of music in this church may be to the glory of God,

PEOPLE: We dedicate this organ.

MINISTER: To the glory of God, the Father Almighty, that we may the more worthily worship him,

PEOPLE: We dedicate this organ.

MINISTER: To the glory of Jesus Christ, the Saviour of the world, at whose coming to earth the multitude of the heavenly host sang the song of the ages, "Glory to God in the highest, and on earth peace, good will toward men," that our joy in him may find the more worthy expression,

PEOPLE: We dedicate this organ.

MINISTER: To the Holy Spirit, in whose fellowship the discords of life are lost in the glorious harmony of God, that we may more fully interpret his promptings in our minds ond hearts.

PEOPLE: We dedicate this organ.

MINISTER: To the church of Jesus Christ and its mission in the world; the comforting of the sorrowful, the strengthening of the weak, the cheering of the weary, the curing of the sin-sick souls, the swelling of the chorus of praise,

PEOPLE: We dedicate this organ.

MINISTER: To the cause of greater religious fervor and a

[17] As used by the Emanuel A.M.E. Church, Portsmouth, Virginia; Charles H. Stewart was the minister at the time.

deeper appreciation of the sacred hymns which came as profound expressions from the very souls of the God inspired,

PEOPLE: We dedicate these chimes.

MINISTER: For the ministry of music to the soul; for inspiration to praise through heart-touching melodies and majestic harmonies,

PEOPLE: We dedicate these chimes.

MINISTER: For the awakening of the spirit of devotion, for the soothing of troubled hearts in anxiety, for the giving of cheer to the downcast and of comfort to the sorrowing, and for the kindling of courage and of high and holy purpose in those who hear them,

PEOPLE: We dedicate these chimes.

MINISTER: For the humbling of the heart in awe before the eternal mysteries, for the thrilling of the soul with joy by the message of infinite love, for the exaltation of the soul in rapture before the promised victory of life triumphant,

PEOPLE: We dedicate these chimes.

PRAYER OF DEDICATION

MINISTER: Our heavenly Father, we beseech thee to accept this organ and these chimes as a token of our love for thee and of our desire to praise and magnify thy holy name.

PEOPLE: AMEN.

MINISTER: If it be thy divine will, may the melodies produced through this organ and these chimes be the source through which men shall call thy name blessed.

PEOPLE: AMEN.

MINISTER: May this organ and these chimes serve to disperse the darkness of evil and illuminate the paths of those who walk in darkness by the comfort their strains shall give and the hope their music shall proclaim.

PEOPLE: AMEN.

MINISTER: May those who listen be lifted to high inspiration and, being inspired, see more clearly their tasks in the valley of benighted men and human misery.

PEOPLE: AMEN.

MINISTER: Accept, gracious Lord, this work of our hands and the worship of our hearts and the songs of our souls.

PEOPLE: AMEN.

MINISTER: Translate our lives into the notes and modulations of thy life, cheer and inspire us by all thy ministries, and may all the strains of our earthly praise find their harmony in the great chorus of those who sing around the throne of the redeemed forever.

PEOPLE: AMEN.

MINISTER: This we ask in the name of Jesus Christ our Lord.

PEOPLE: AMEN.

RESPONSIVE READING: Ps. 150

Praise ye the Lord. Praise God in his sanctuary: praise him in firmament of his power.

Praise him for his mighty acts: praise him according to his excellent greatness.

Praise him with the sound of the trumpet: praise him with the psaltery and harp.

Praise him with the timbrel and dance: praise him with stringed instruments and organs.

Praise him upon the loud cymbals: praise him with the high sounding cymbals.

Let everything that hath breath praise the Lord.

Praise ye the Lord.

18. THE DEDICATION OF CARILLONIC BELLS [18]

SERVICE OF DEDICATION

Our help is in the name of the Lord,

Who made heaven and earth.

Praise ye the Lord.

Praise God in his sanctuary: praise him in the firmament of His power.

Give unto the Lord the glory due unto his name.

Worship the Lord in the beauty of holiness.

Glory be to the Father, and to the Son, and to the Holy Ghost:

As it was in the beginning, is now, and ever shall be, world without end. AMEN.

The Lord be with you:

And with thy spirit.

[18] As used in St. Paul's Evangelical Lutheran Church, East Port Chester, Connecticut; Frederick W. Grunst is the pastor.

Let us pray:

O God, who by thy servant Moses didst command that silver trumpets should be made to call the people to holy assemblies, bless, we beseech thee, this carillonic tower system, dedicated to thine honor and glory, and grant that its voice may sound forth from generation to generation, ever calling thy children to holy convocation in praise and worship of thy glorious name; through Jesus Christ thy Son, our Lord. AMEN.

WORDS OF DEDICATION

Blest and dedicated be this carillonic tower system to the honor and glory of Almighty God, in the name of the Father, and of the Son, and of the Holy Ghost. AMEN.

Sing forth the honor of his name: make his praise glorious!

Hallowed also be this carillonic tower system as a memorial to ——————————.

The memory of the just is blessed.

INTERCESSORY PRAYER:

Almighty God, who dost endow thy children with manifold gifts and graces, blessing their lives with the treasures of beauty and harmony, and dost make skillful their hands to the creation of the useful and beautiful, accept this our offering which we have dedicated to thy service, and grant that its use may ever be a hallowed one and that its sound may never cease to call men unto thee.

We beseech thee to hear us, O Lord.

We humbly pray its voice may ever be a joyful sound to

thy children, calling them to worship and prayer, that they may enter into thy gates with thanksgiving and into thy courts with praise.

We beseech Thee to hear us, O Lord.

We humbly pray that its voice may ever be a calling to remembrance to those who have strayed from thy way, that it may call in solemn rebuke to the careless and indifferent, that it may ring forth a sure welcome to the sinner and to whosoever will come.

We beseech Thee to hear us, O Lord.

We humbly pray for those who through the sorrows and sufferings of this present life are prevented from coming to thy house, that its sound may bring to mind thy love and compassion for all who suffer, thy courage and help for those who are sore beset, thy peace for those who are heavy laden, and thy comfort for those who mourn.

We beseech Thee to hear us, O Lord.

We humbly pray that when a soul passes forth into the life that knows no ending, its voice may proclaim to all the glorious victory which our Lord Jesus Christ, thy son, hath obtained for us and for all who sleep in him; that hearing, we may be led to seek thy grace, and so live that we may enter into the rest prepared for the children of God.

We beseech Thee to hear us, O Lord.

And when it sounds forth far and wide in rejoicing and thanksgiving, may we lift up our hearts in adoration and praise to thee, O God, the Father, the Son, and the Holy Ghost, who livest and reignest evermore. AMEN.

19. A SERVICE FOR THE DEDICATION
OF CHOIR VESTMENTS—I [19]

MINISTER: O come, let us sing unto the Lord: let us make a joyful noise to the rock of our salvation.

PEOPLE: Let us come before his presence with thanksgiving, and make a joyful noise unto him with psalms.

MINISTER: O sing unto the Lord a new song: for he hath done marvelous things: his right hand, and his holy arm, hath gotten him the victory.

PEOPLE: Make a joyful noise unto the Lord, all the earth: . . . rejoice, and sing praise.

MINISTER: Sing unto the Lord with the harp; with the harp, and the voice of a psalm.

PEOPLE: I will sing unto the Lord as long as I live: I will sing praises to my God while I have my being.

MINISTER: Sing unto him, sing psalms unto him: talk ye of all his wondrous works.

PEOPLE: I will sing a new song unto thee, O God: upon a psaltery and an instrument of ten strings will I sing praises unto thee.

MINISTER: Let every thing that hath breath praise the Lord.

PEOPLE: Praise God in his sanctuary: praise him in the firmament of his power. . . . Praise ye the Lord.

READER: The choirs of a church are invaluable. During the acts of worship the choir has many opportunities for leadership and guidance. The choir sings with the congregation on the hymns, leads in the responsive scrip-

[19] As used in West Creighton Avenue Christian Church, Fort Wayne, Indiana. The program was planned by the minister, Russell E. Palmer.

ture readings, and in the attitudes of prayer. The choirs thus supply tonal, rhythmical, and intellectual guidance.

They sing for the congregation. Here the people, unable to join in the higher forms of anthem, chorale, and responses, sing silently, while choristers audibly voice prayer and praise, yearning and ecstasies. For this vicarious act, singers should take the vows of loyalty, humility, and dedication, for only those of clean hands and pure hearts may rightly lift to the throne of grace the petitions and thanksgivings of a worshiping people.

In singing to the congregation, the choir renders a personal service as comforter and exhorter to teach each and every layman. Thus music is no longer a profession but a principle, with the singer an evangelist, with discerning instinct and sustained fervor, imparting his faith to others.

Choirs should emulate the masters of tone who knew God and served him. Beethoven said, "God looks into my heart. He searches it and knows that love for man and feelings for benevolence have their abode there." Bach said, "The sole end and aim of thoroughness, like that of all music, should be nothing else than the glory of God and pleasant recreation." Handel as he was writing the "Hallelujah Chorus" of *The Messiah* said, "I did think I did see all heaven before me and the great God himself."

The choir robe has been worn in the church for many centuries. The surplice came into existence around the eleventh century and was worn strictly as a choir vestment. In the beginning it was a full length garment, but began to be shortened around the fifteenth century. The appearance of a vested choir does much for the church and the congregation. It is restful for them. It avoids the undesirable distraction so often caused by variety of dress in the choir. It also contributes to the simplicity of effect and leads the congregation in concentration on worship. All of these are highly desirable as we worship together.

LITANY OF DEDICATION

MINISTER: To the glory of God and to the singing of praises to his holy name,

PEOPLE: We dedicate these robes.

MINISTER: To the enrichment of our corporate worship experience,

PEOPLE: We dedicate these robes.

MINISTER: To the end that we may forget human personality and see only God in the music of our worship service,

PEOPLE: We dedicate these robes.

MINISTER: To the end that unity and harmony of human voices blended together into a choir might portray to us the personal unity and harmony that is possible with God,

PEOPLE: We dedicate these robes.

MINISTER: To the holy purposes of God revealed to us in the worship experience of the church, drawing us into a more intimate, personal relationship with God, Christ, and the Holy Spirit,

PEOPLE: We dedicate these robes.

PRAYER OF DEDICATION (unison)

O Lord, our God, whose name is excellent and whose glory is above the earth and heaven; we beseech thee to bless these thy servants who sing praises to thy holy name and these robes that they are wearing. To them has been given the sacred trust of leading the praises of thy people in the sanctuary. As thou hast called them to this, thy service, make and keep them worthy of this calling. Let the Holy Spirit rule in their hearts as they carry out this sacred trust. May they lead others to offer their worship in reverence, and to sing with the understanding and the heart, as unto thee and not unto men. Grant that they may be as one with thy people in their love for thy house and their fellowship in thy service, that all of us may find joy and increase of faith in praising thy wonderful and holy name.

Bless these vestments and the holy purposes to which they are dedicated this day. Bless the ones in whose precious memory they are given to our church. Bless those who wear these robes through the years, that they may never lose sight of this gracious privilege coming to them from our God. In thy great mercy grant that all who learn here to find joy in worshiping thee may be numbered at last with those who shall sing a new song before thy heavenly throne; through Jesus Christ our Lord, who is worshiped and glorified, with thee, O Father, and the Holy Spirit, world without end. AMEN.

20. A SERVICE OF DEDICATION OF CHOIR VESTMENTS—II [20]

MINISTER: Dearly beloved, inasmuch as new vestments have been purchased for the choir of this church, it is fitting that we pause and dedicate them to the glory of Almighty God, and to pray that he will bless us in the future use of them. May his smile of approval be upon us now and evermore.

MINISTER: That those who worship here shall, through the ministry of music, learn of thy great love and commit their lives unto thee,

PEOPLE: We earnestly and fervently pray to thee, O Lord of Hosts.

MINISTER: That, as we come before thee with songs of praise, thou wilt abundantly bless,

PEOPLE: We earnestly pray to thee, O Lord, our rock and our hope.

MINISTER: That all who worship here shall be inspired and comforted and realize thy presence through the ministry of sacred music,

PEOPLE: We humbly pray and beseech thee, O Lord, our God.

[20] Compiled by G. R. Bright, Methodist Church, Philippi, West Virginia.

MINISTER: That we shall not forget those whose labors of yesterday bless us today,

PEOPLE: May we never forget these, Lord of heaven and of earth,

MINISTER: That we recognize and appreciate these who give a ministry of labor and love in our midst today,

PEOPLE: We are grateful to thee for these, O Lord, and beseech thee to give unto them a blessing.

MINISTER: That by proper use of these vestments this church shall increase in power, in praise, and in lofty purpose to promote thy kingdom in this world,

PEOPLE: We consecrate these vestments to the development of thy kingdom, O Lord.

MINISTER: That as we behold these vestments in days to come, the love for the church—our spiritual mother— shall be quickened, and the new loyalty pledged unto her,

PEOPLE: We dedicate these vestments to this high and holy purpose, O Lord, our God.

MINISTER: That the gospel shall come to us by sacred melody, as well as by the preached word,

PEOPLE: We dedicate these vestments unto thee, O Lord, our Savior and Friend.

PRAYER (*unison*)

O thou God of beauty and order, we pray that thou will accept this the work of our hands which we now bring to thee. May no careless word or act ever detract from the holy purpose to which we have dedicated these vestments. Be thou always with those who shall wear these, and through their ministry bless thou this church, through Jesus Christ, our Lord. AMEN.

MINISTER: As minister of this church, I hereby dedicate these choir vestments to the glory of Almighty God, and to the promotion of his kingdom. In the name of the Father, Son, and Holy Spirit. AMEN.

21. THE DEDICATION OF CHURCH HYMNALS [21]

MINISTER: These new hymnals are the gifts of a large number of members and friends of this church. So as we solemnly dedicate them to God, we also express our appreciation to those who have so lovingly given them,

PEOPLE: **It is a good thing to give thanks unto the Lord, and to sing praises unto thy name, O most High. (Ps. 92:1.)**

MINISTER: Let the word of Christ dwell in you richly in all wisdom; teaching and admonishing one another in psalms and hymns and spiritual songs, singing with grace in your hearts to the Lord. (Col. 3:16.)

PEOPLE: **And when they had sung an hymn, they went out into the Mount of Olives. (Matt. 26:30.)**

MINISTER: Sing unto the Lord a new song, and his praise from the end of the earth. (Isa. 42:10.)

PEOPLE: **And they sung as it were a new song before the**

---

[21] As arranged by Louis V. S. Hutton and used at the First Baptist Church, Catskill, New York.

throne, . . . and the elders . . . which were redeemed from the earth. (Rev. 14:3.)

MINISTER: To the glory of God who was living when the morning stars sang together,

PEOPLE: We dedicate these hymnals.

MINISTER: To the honor of Jesus Christ at whose birth the angels sang,

PEOPLE: We dedicate these hymnals.

MINISTER: To the praise of the Holy Spirit in whose fellowship the discords of life are lost in perfect harmony,

PEOPLE: We dedicate these hymnals.

MINISTER: To the memory of those who in days gone by labored in this church,

PEOPLE: We dedicate these hymnals.

MINISTER: For the quickening of the spiritual life of our church, and the kindling of courage and devotion,

PEOPLE: We dedicate these hymnals.

ALL: For the comfort of the sorrowing, the strengthening of the weak, the cheering of the weary, for help in singing the songs of Zion, we, the people of this church dedicate these books and ourselves to the service of God and man, in the name of Christ our rightful Master. AMEN.

PRAYER (unison)

We thank thee, our Father, for those whose many gifts made possible these new books. We pray that we may go work together and with thee, that through us, thou canst

99

do greater things for thy church and thy kingdom. In Christ's name we ask it. AMEN.

22. THE DEDICATION OF MEMORIAL BIBLES [22]

MINISTER: In honor of God our Father who created us and gave to us the priceless gift of speech,

PEOPLE: We dedicate these Bibles.

MINISTER: In praise of Jesus Christ, the Incarnate Word, who spoke with matchless power and grace,

PEOPLE: We dedicate these Bibles.

MINISTER: In remembrance of the Holy Spirit, who speaks to the hidden things in men's hearts,

PEOPLE: We dedicate these Bibles.

MINISTER: In loving memory of ————————————,

PEOPLE: We dedicate these Bibles.

MINISTER AND PEOPLE (unison): To the glory of God, the enlightenment of this congregation, the strengthening of the ties which bind us to all men, these Bibles are now dedicated. May humble tongues proclaim their imperishable truths and receptive hearts receive the messages they impart. AMEN.

HYMN: "For All the Saints"

[22] As used in the First Reformed Church, Passaic, New Jersey; Millard M. Gifford, minister.

PRAYER

All wise God, who dost raise up men of faith in every generation to serve thee and dost imbue them with godliness and human qualities of unusual worth, we thank thee for thy servant, _____. He (she) was devout in faith, affectionate in spirit, loyal to vows, steadfast in duty. He (she) loved thee because he (she) knew that every spirit came from thee; he (she) loved Jesus Christ for to him (her) he was the hope of the world, the friend of all mankind; he (she) loved this church for he (she) felt that it was a house of prayer for all people. O God, on this day when we meditate upon the spirits of just men made perfect, make us grateful for his (her) gentle and compassionate ministry of life and talents. May thy presence continually be felt by his (her) loved ones and by us, providing all with faith, with courage and the hope of eternal life, through Jesus Christ, our Lord. AMEN.

23. THE DEDICATION OF A STAINED-GLASS WINDOW—I [23]

MINISTER: He shall feed his flock like a shepherd; he shall gather the lambs in his arm and carry them in his bosom, and shall gently lead those that are with young. Behold the lamb of God which taketh away the sins of the world.

[23] As used in Bethany Presbyterian Church, Flint, Michigan, E. G. Black, minister.

MINISTER: Eternal God, who didst inspire artists of thine ancient church and tabernacle to adorn thy house of prayer with splendid color and rich ornament; thou who hast created stones with fair colors such as the agate, the sapphire, the ruby, and the carbuncle; who hast painted the earth with green and brown and red and all the gorgeous colors of the rainbow,

PEOPLE: To thee, O God, we dedicate this window.

MINISTER: To the ministry of art to the soul of man, for the inspiration of the design of this window to the intellect and for the direction of the thoughts of the congregation in channels of Christian meditations,

PEOPLE: We dedicate this window.

MINISTER: For the beneficent influence of the figure of Christ upon the youth of our church and for the quiet, unobtrusive effect upon all who worship here or who pass through this sanctuary; that little children, young pople, and adults may be led to accept the teachings of the Good Shepherd and become his disciples,

PEOPLE: We dedicate this window.

MINISTER: For the creative skill of artist and craftsman, and their ability to capture in pigment and glass, in wood and stone, the eternal and the imperishable,

PEOPLE: We give thee thanks, O Lord.

MINISTER: For all who have labored and served and sacrificed that this window might be made possible, which in an age of moral ugliness and conflict reminds us of all that is good and beautiful and true, and of him who is altogether lovely and the fairest among ten thousand,

PEOPLE: O Lord our God, accept our thanks.

MINISTER: To the glory of God the Father, to the service of Jesus Christ and his church, and to the quickening influence and guidance of his Holy Spirit, who ever seeks to dwell in the temple of men's hearts and lives,

PEOPLE: We dedicate this window, in the name of the Father, Son, and Holy Ghost. AMEN.

PRAYER OF DEDICATION (*unison*)

O thou who art the creator of all things and all men, we thank thee for the genius of men, for the spirit of sacrifice, for the love of the beautiful in men's souls which they have transferred to this, thy sanctuary. May we ever find here that uplift of spirit and that renewed faith which will bring forth fruit with patience and with love, to the glory of Jesus Christ our Lord. AMEN.

24. THE DEDICATION OF A STAINED-GLASS WINDOW—II [24]

MINISTER: O thou eternal spirit who has put it into the hearts of men to worship thee and to erect places consecrated to the expression of their love and loyalty, we thank thee for this sanctuary dedicated to thine honor and glory.

[24] As used in the Second Presbyterian Church, Oswegatchie, New York.

Hear our words of gratitude and dedication as we offer this stained-glass window for the adorning and beautifying of this church.

CHOIR: Thou art the king of glory, O Christ; thou art the everlasting Son of the Father.

MINISTER: For beauty so lavishly spread over this earth, whereby we are reminded of thy beauty and discern thy loving presence,

POEPLE: O God, we thank thee.

MINISTER: For the stimulus that comes to the mind and personality of man through the fascination of light and shadow, color, lines, and forms; through the inspiration of design and symbol,

PEOPLE: Creator of all loveliness, we thank thee.

MINISTER: For the creative skill of artist and craftsman and their ability to capture in stone and wood, glass and pigment, the eternal and imperishable,

PEOPLE: We give thee thanks, O God.

MINISTER: For all those whose gifts have made possible this stained-glass window, which in an age of conflict and strife reminds us of all that is good and true and beautiful,

PEOPLE: O Lord our God, accept our thanks.

MINISTER: To the glory of God the Father, to the service of Jesus Christ and his church, and to the quickening influence and guidance of his holy spirit, whoever seeks to dwell within the temple of our hearts,

PEOPLE: We dedicate this window.

MINISTER: For the purpose that this window may beautify and glorify this sanctuary, influencing the meditations of all who worship here; that it may inspire little children, young people and adults to accept his teachings and become his disciples,

PEOPLE: We dedicate this window.

PRAYER (unison)

Almighty God, who has inspired men of all time to adorn the place of worship with splendid color, rich design, and choicest art, grant that this window may assist our faith and inspire our purpose to love thee more by serving our fellow men. We know that thou dwellest not in temples made with hands but with those who are of a humble and contrite heart. Grant therefore, we beseech thee, that the rich beauty of this window may inspire all who behold it to more Christlike living. In his spirit we pray. AMEN.

25. THE DEDICATION OF A SERVICE HONOR ROLL [25]

MINISTER: Eternal Father, from whom comes every good and perfect gift, and by whose inspiration men have won kingdoms and wrought righteousness, hear us in mercy as we meet around our common altar to raise to thee our litany of dedication.

[25] Arranged by J. Richmond Morgan, First Congregational Church, Peru, Illinois.

In proud and affectionate memory of our sons and daughters who have been accounted worthy to be called to the honorable service of our nation,

UNISON: **We dedicate this roll of honor.**

MINISTER: In the persuasion that the cause they serve is worthy of their highest allegiance, and that in sending forth its youth this church is helping to fulfill thy purpose for the world,

UNISON: **We dedicate this roll of honor.**

MINISTER: In the assurance that the ideals they seek to preserve are thine, that their defense is essential for the continuance of thy kingdom, and that they are worthy of our utmost sacrifice,

UNISON: **We dedicate this roll of honor.**

MINISTER: In the confidence that thou dost call us to share with thee in the sacrificial cost of maintaining the privileges won for us by our venerable forebears,

UNISON: **We dedicate this roll of honor.**

MINISTER: In simple faith that he who taught us that life is more than meat, and that no sparrow falls unnoticed, will watch over our patriot children,

UNISON: **We dedicate this roll of honor.**

MINISTER: To the honor of all those who have answered the call of duty, who labor for truth and freedom, and who offer their sacrifice as the price of a better world,

UNISON: **We dedicate this roll of honor.**

UNISON: **Grant us, O God, as we seek to preserve the memory of those whom now we honor, that we may** be quickened to unselfish devotion to our common cause, and that putting away all inordinate ease and slothful indulgence we may we worthy of our heritage, and faithful to the best traditions of our faith and nation. AMEN.

CHANT RESPONSE: "The Lord's Prayer"

PRAYER (Minister)

Eternal God, thou pitying judge and father of all mankind, on this hour dedicated to the memory of those who represent us in the world's great conflict, hear as our hearts beat out to thee the things that are unutterable and as we sob the latent breathings of our souls.

Thou knowest our needs. Thou seest how difficult it is to live happily and hopefully in a world where all our dear, accustomed ways grow doubtful and insecure. Be thou our help, for we cannot do much for our fellows if we ourselves are undone. Keep us close to the eternal sources, and as from some cool fountain from the hidden deeps nourish us with faith, hope, and courage, that we may know that inner calm that comes to those whose hearts are stayed on thee.

We raise to thee our deep concern for the world. In mercy remember the youth of our day, burdened and harassed by such huge demands that they might well lose all high hope and valid faith. Protect them, O Father, with love of God. Raise up from their ranks those who will redress their wrongs and lead them back to ways of blessedness and peace.

Witness our sorrow for the prejudice that blows its ill will across the world, and forgive us as we repent the stupidity that choose war rather than peace, suspicion when we might have trust.

As we bow in proud grief before the names of those who gave their lives in glad, abandoned sacrifice, we repent in shame that such sacrifice should ever become necessary. This is our sin, O God, the sin of us all, that we should have worked for peace without reference to thee or to thy holy will. Forgive us as in our desperation we pray for thy peace and for our rededication to all good cause that keeps the peace.

Let the impact of thy power be upon thy church. Keep it sane that it may bring sanity back to the world. Make it wise that it may make men wiser. Make it good that it may always and everywhere insist on goodness. Grant, O Merciful Father, that the waiting world may find in thy church a new dedication to all that makes for peace, brotherhood, righteousness, and the spirit of Jesus Christ, our rightful Lord and Master. AMEN.

HYMN: "The Son of God Goes Forth to War." Tune, "All Saints"

"God Save America." Tune, "Russian Hymn"

26. THE DEDICATION OF CHRISTIAN AND NATIONAL FLAGS—I [26]

If the special music is to be built around the theme of "God and Patriotism," we would suggest for the choir, "Anthem of Democracy," by J. H. Matthews,[27] "O Lord God of Hosts, Strengthen and Guide This Nation," by Gaul, and "Recessional" by H. A. Matthews.[28]

DEDICATION SERVICE

PEOPLE: In the name of the Father and of the Son, and of the Holy Spirit. AMEN.

MINISTER: To the glory of God and to our spiritual enrichment,

PEOPLE: To thee, we dedicate these flags.

MINISTER: That all who enter this house of God may be reminded of the atoning life and death of our Lord, Jesus Christ,

PEOPLE: To thee, we dedicate this church flag.

MINISTER: That all who worship here may be reminded of the religious freedom and tolerance for which it stands,

PEOPLE: To thee, we dedicate this American flag.

MINISTER: That its presence here may help to keep us close to him in whom alone we have hope of life and happiness,

PEOPLE: To thee, we dedicate this church flag.

MINISTER: That constantly we may thank God for the

[26] A service arranged by John Alexander Hayes and used by him in the dedicatory service at the First Presbyterian Church, Red Bank, New Jersey.
[27] H. W. Gray Co.
[28] Schirmer.

sacrificial service of those who endured hardship and suffering to bring it into being,

PEOPLE: To thee, we dedicate this American flag.

MINISTER: That silently side by side during each service, they may remind us of our duty to God and country, of the love of our Savior and of the freedom of our nation,

PEOPLE: To thee, we dedicate these flags.

DEDICATORY PRAYER

SALUTE TO THE CHURCH FLAG

I pledge allegiance to the Christian flag and to the Saviour for whose kingdom it stands; one brotherhood uniting all mankind in service and love.

PEOPLE (*singing*)

"Our father's God to Thee,
Author of liberty,
　　To Thee we sing;
Long may our land be bright
With freedom's holy light;
Protect us by Thy might;
　　Great God, our King."

SALUTE TO THE AMERICAN FLAG

I pledge allegiance to the flag of the United States of America and to the republic for which it stands; one nation, under God, indivisible, with liberty and justice for all.

PEOPLE (*singing*)

> "My native country, thee
> Land of the noble, free,
>   Thy name I love;
> I love thy rocks and rills,
> Thy woods and templed hills;
> My heart with rapture thrills,
>   Like that above."

27. THE DEDICATION OF CHRISTIAN AND NATIONAL FLAGS—II [29]

PRESENTATION OF THE FLAGS

I present to the Church the Christian flag and the American flag.

ACCEPTANCE OF THE FLAG

As minister, on behalf of the congregation, I accept these flags to their sacred and patriotic use.

DEDICATION OF THE FLAGS

MINISTER: To the glory of God and our spiritual enrichment,

PEOPLE: We dedicate the Christian flag.

MINISTER: As a symbol of him, who said: Follow me,

PEOPLE: We dedicate the Christian flag.

---

[29] As used in the Evangelical Congregational Church, McKeesport, Pennsylvania. John F. C. Green is the minister of the church.

MINISTER: That this emblem of our country may bring to our minds the watchful providence of the God who guards his faithful people,

PEOPLE: **We dedicate this American flag.**

MINISTER: As a hallowed reminder of the sacrifices in loyalty of those who have faithfully served our country, and as the expression of the highest patriotism of her people,

PEOPLE: **We dedicate this American flag.**

THE PLEDGE OF ALLEGIANCE

I pledge allegiance to the Christian flag and to the Saviour for whose kingdom it stands; one brotherhood uniting all mankind in service and love.

I pledge allegiance to the flag of the United States of America and to the republic for which it stands; one nation, under God, indivisible, with liberty and justice for all.

SONG

Our fathers' God, to Thee
Author of liberty,
To Thee we sing;
Long may our land be bright
With freedom's holy light;
Protect us by Thy might;
Great God, our King. AMEN.

28. THE DEDICATION OF A PROJECTOR [30]

MINISTER: That we might increase our knowledge of our Lord and his ministry and to know the true meaning of discipleship,

PEOPLE: We dedicate this sound projector.

MINISTER: That we might come to a better understanding of the world and its peoples and lay the foundations for peace,

PEOPLE: We dedicate this sound projector.

MINISTER: That we might become aware of the beauties of God's world which we are unable to visit,

PEOPLE: We dedicate this sound projector.

MINISTER: That we might come to a better understanding of the total missionary program of our church and be more willing to give,

PEOPLE: We dedicate this sound projector.

MINISTER: That we might come to know the truths by which men shall be free,

PEOPLE: We dedicate this sound projector.

MINISTER: That we might enhance the spirit of fellowship by the use of this equipment in the social life of the church,

PEOPLE: We dedicate this sound projector.

MINISTER: That through the directed use of this equipment we may be led to a better vision of the lives we can live and the world that can be,

PEOPLE: We dedicate this equipment to the glory of God and the ministry of our church.

[30] As used in Trinity United Church, North Bay, Ontario, Canada.

DEDICATION PRAYER

Almighty God, we pray for thy guidance in the use of this equipment that through our lives consecrated to thy kingdom's cause it shall serve thee and the people. May we be endowed with new power of righteousness in its use. May we come to a better understanding of thy work, of our Lord and his ministry to a needy world; of thy world and thy people everywhere. May we be knit closer together in fellowship as we dedicate this equipment to thy glory and honor. AMEN.

DUET: "Open Our Eyes"

29. THE DEDICATION OF A BOOK
OF REMEMBRANCE [31]

OPENING HYMN: "O God, Our Help in Ages Past"

LITANY OF DEDICATION

MINISTER: Dearly beloved, we are gathered together here in reverence and sincerity to dedicate a book of remembrance for relatives, friends, and fellow members who answered the call of our country in her hour of emergency. Name by name, we shall enter them on this record. Name by name, we shall keep them in our hearts and in our prayers.

MINISTER: In order that we may not be unrighteous to forget the freedom for which our forefathers died,

[31] Adapted from a service used in the First Pilgrim Congregational Church, Buffalo, New York.

PEOPLE: We dedicate this book.

MINISTER: As a testimony that neither distance nor death has dominion over our Christian fellowship,

PEOPLE: We dedicate this book.

MINISTER: In recognition of the redeeming power of sacrifice and innocent suffering,

PEOPLE: We dedicate this book.

MINISTER: As a pledge of lasting friendship, affection, and gratitude to those of our own who have answered the call of our country,

PEOPLE: We dedicate this book.

MINISTER: As a covenant that we shall, under God, do what we can for the establishment of peace and freedom and good will throughout the earth so that they should have not fought and died in vain,

PEOPLE: We dedicate this book.

MINISTER: In the name of the Father and of the Son and of the Holy Spirit,

PEOPLE: We dedicate this book.

LIGHTING OF THE CANDLES

SOLO: "Recessional," DeKovin

PRAYER

CLOSING HYMN: O God, Our Help in Ages Past
O God, our help, in ages past,
Our hope for years to come,

Our shelter from the stormy blast,
And our eternal home!

Before the hills in order stood,
Or earth received her frame,
From everlasting Thou art God,
To endless years the same.

A thousand ages in Thy sight,
Are like an evening gone;
Short as the watch that ends the night,
Before the rising sun.

O God, our help, in ages past,
Our hope for years to come,
Be Thou our guide while life shall last,
And our eternal home!

ISAAC WATTS

BENEDICTION

30. THE DEDICATION OF A
BULLETIN BOARD [32]

MINISTER: "Give ear, O ye heavens, and I will speak; and hear, O earth, the words of my mouth.

"My doctrine shall drop as the rain, my speech shall distil as the dew, as the small rain upon the tender herb, and as the showers upon the grass:

[32] As used at the First Baptist Church, Woburn, Massachusetts.

"Because I will publish the name of the Lord: ascribe ye greatness unto our God." (Deut. 32:1-3.)

"Declare ye in Judah, and publish in Jerusalem, and say, Blow ye the trumpet in the land: cry, gather together, and say, Assemble yourselves." (Jer. 4:5.)

"Ye are the light of the world. A city that is set upon a hill cannot be hid.

"Neither do men light a candle, and put it under a bushel, but on a candlestick; and it giveth light unto all that are in the house.

"Let your light so shine before men, that they may see your good works, and glorify your Father which is in heaven." (Matt. 5:14-16.)

(The congregation will rise.)

MINISTER: From without and above comes to man the call to worship God, and from deep down in man's heart rises the response. Let this bulletin remind men of the object of worship, and invite them to share the blessings of worship in the house of God.

PEOPLE: AMEN.

MINISTER: Not unto themselves should men live. For God and humanity should they bend their efforts remembering well the "Eleventh Commandment" respecting love to God and one's neighbor. Let this bulletin from time to time reveal that Christians are engaged unselfishly in the service of God and man.

PEOPLE: AMEN.

MINISTER: Together are worthwhile aims achieved as this present work testifies. Endearing and enduring is the fellowship of a common task. So, too, is the fellowship of recreation and pleasure. Let this bulletin declare that only together in well-balanced activity can each realize his noblest, highest self.

PEOPLE: AMEN.

MINISTER: Let us pray. (*Offer prayer.*)

(*The congregation will be seated after prayer.*)

31. THE DEDICATION OF A WAYSIDE MEMORIAL BULLETIN BOARD [33]

(*Congregation Standing*)

MINISTER: And God said, let there be light,

PEOPLE: And there was light.

MINISTER: The gospel which we proclaim is "good news." From the days of the early church many devices have been used to publish this good news—the pulpit, religious symbols, song, the printed page. This outdoor bulletin board which we now dedicate is in a distinguished succession. As a wayside pulpit, proclaiming day and night to passers-by the good news of the Christian faith,

PEOPLE: We dedicate this bulletin board.

MINISTER: That all who pass this may have an invitation to worship God and to experience the warmth of Christian fellowship,

[33] As used by the Cleveland Park Congregational Church, Washington, D.C.; Alfred W. Hurst, minister.

PEOPLE: We dedicate this bulletin board.

MINISTER: Not unto themselves should men live but unto God and humanity. To reveal from time to time that the church is engaged in unselfish service of God and man,

PEOPLE: We dedicate this bulletin board.

MINISTER: That a well-balanced program of fellowship, recreation, and social pleasure designed to help people realize their noblest and highest selves, may be made known,

PEOPLE: We dedicate this bulletin board.

MINISTER: To the enlightenment of this community through the great spirit of truth which alone can make men free,

PEOPLE: We dedicate this bulletin board.

PRAYER OF DEDICATION

O God, today we dedicate a wayside pulpit in memory of one whose personality proclaimed the eloquence of goodness. We dedicate it to a holy service that the good news of the gospel of Christ may be proclaimed. Through it may minds be enlightened, hearts comforted, and steps directed to works of righteousness, love, and truth, according to thy holy will. As this memorial bulletin stands untarnished in strength and beauty, may lives be drawn toward the life over which time has no power. Beyond our power to dedicate wilt thou consecrate us all that we may help make thy world the dwelling place of light. Through Jesus Christ our Lord. AMEN.

III
OTHER DEDICATIONS

1. THE DEDICATION OF A MANSE [1]

SCRIPTURE SALUTATION: Ps. 103:1-2

Bless the Lord, O my soul: and all that is within me, bless his holy name. Bless the Lord, O my soul, and forget not all his benefits.

A HOUSE OF HAPPINESS

Happy is the family that has a true home, built by loyal hearts; for home is not a dwelling, but a living fellowship, and when people dwell together with understanding and affection, they make their home a house of happiness.

It takes a heap o' livin' in a house t' make it home,
A heap o' sun an' shadder, an' ye sometimes have t' roam
Afore ye really 'preciate the things ye lef' behind,
An' hunger fer 'em somehow, with 'em allus on yer mind.
It don't make any differunce how rich ye get t' be,
How much yer chairs an' tables cost, how great yer luxury;
It ain't home t' ye, though it be the palace of a king,
Until somehow yer soul is sort o' wrapped round everything.

Home ain't a place that gold can buy or get up in a minute;
Afore it's home, there's got t' be a heap o' livin' in it;

[1] Adapted from the dedication of the Presbyterian manse, Bay Village, Ohio. The service was compiled by Franklin P. Reinhold, pastor emeritus of the church.

Within the walls there's got t' be some babies born, and then
Right there ye've got t' bring 'em up t' women good, an' men;

. . . .

Ye've got t' weep t' make it home, ye've got t' sit an' sigh
An' watch beside a loved one's bed, an' know that Death is nigh.[2]

EDGAR A. GUEST

PRESENTATION OF THE PROPERTY FOR DEDICATION BY THE CHURCH OFFICERS

We, the officers of the _____ Church of _____, and in behalf of the members of our congregation, do hereby present this manse for dedication as a home for you and your family, and for the ministers of our church in the future. We present this manse to be dedicated to the glory of God, and for the building of Christian home life in our village.

ACCEPTANCE BY THE MINISTER

In recognition of the privilege so generously provided by the officers and members of _____ Church of _____, we who make up this minister's family most gratefully accept this manse as our home and gladly join you in this meaningful act of dedication.

[2] From "Home"—*Collected Verse of Edgar A. Guest*, Copyright 1934, The Reilly & Lee Company.

(*All uniting*): Trusting in the Lord Jesus Christ for strength, we therefore unite in this act of dedication.

In the name of the Father, and of the Son, and of the Holy Spirit we dedicate this manse to God.

We dedicate this manse to work and leisure, to serious thought and to lightsome laughter, to love and comradeship, to courtesy and mutual understanding, to loyalty and high fellowship.

We dedicate this manse to the services of God and man as a unit of the kingdom of God, believing that the kingdom will come in our village and in the world when enough homes, and the children of these homes, seek to do the will of their heavenly Father.

Thus with grateful minds and hearts to Almighty God and relying upon his strength to help us, we dedicate this manse.

PRAYER OF DEDICATION

Lord, bless this house of brick and wood,
This home of love and care.
Bless those who make these walls a home;
Receive their daily prayer.

Let love and joy sustain this home;
Give patience to those who wait.
May children's feet find happiness
As they play within its gate.

We pray that those who here may live
Can banish hate and strife

And find within these friendly rooms
    The holy path to life.

THE LORD'S PRAYER

Our Father which art in heaven, Hallowed be thy name. Thy kingdom come. Thy will be done in earth, as it is in heaven. Give us this day our daily bread. And forgive us our debts, as we forgive our debtors. And lead us not into temptation, but deliver us from evil: For thine is the kingdom, and the power, and the glory, for ever. AMEN.

BENEDICTION

The Lord bless us and keep us; the Lord make His face to shine upon us and be gracious unto us; the Lord lift up His countenance upon us and give us peace. In the name of the Father, and of the Son, and of the Holy Spirit. AMEN.

2. THE DEDICATION OF A PARSONAGE [2]

DOXOLOGY (Congregation)

RECOGNITION

MINISTER: "Behold, I stand at the door, and knock: if

---

[2] As used in the Methodist Church, Dayton, Iowa; M. E. Dorr, minister.

any man hear my voice, and open the door, I will come in."

We recognize Christ as the head of this house, its guest and also its Lord.

(*The minister would not normally be the leader of this program; it might be some denominational official, a neighboring clergyman, or a layman who represents the congregation.*)

LEADER: Ye are no more strangers and foreigners, but fellow-citizens with the saints, and of the household of God.

PEOPLE: **And are built upon the foundation of the apostles and prophets, Jesus Christ himself being the chief corner stone.**

LEADER: In whom all the building fitly framed together groweth unto an holy temple in the Lord.

PEOPLE: **In whom ye also are builded together for an habitation of God through the Spirit.**

LEADER: I, therefore, . . . beseech you that ye walk worthy of the vocation wherewith ye were called, with all lowliness and meekness, with longsuffering, forbearing one another in love,

PEOPLE: **Endeavouring to keep the unity of the Spirit in the bond of peace.**

LEADER: Till we all attain unto the unity of the faith, and of the knowledge of the Son of God, unto a full-grown man,

PEOPLE: **Unto the measure of the stature of the fullness of Christ.**

127

LEADER: That we be no longer children, tossed to and fro and carried about with every wind of doctrine, by the sleight of men, in craftiness, after the wiles of error.

PEOPLE: **But speaking truth in love, may grow up in all things unto him who is the head, even Christ.**

PRESIDENT OF THE BOARD OF TRUSTEES: Presentation of keys for parsonage to the minister

MINISTER'S RESPONSE

POEM: "A New House," Isabelle Bryans Longfellow

SOLO: "Bless This House," Brahe

DECLARATION

HUSBAND: We who make up this family believe that God has brought us together and that he is our helper.

WIFE: We agree to work and pray that this home may be a source of strength and a place of warmth and fellowship to all who come into it.

DEDICATION AND CANDLE-LIGHTING LITANY

MEMBER OF SUNDAY SCHOOL: We dedicate this home to love and understanding. May its joys and sorrows be shared and the individuality of each member appreciated. We light a candle to family love.

PEOPLE: **With the help of God and our co-operation we dedicate this home to family love.**

CHILD: We dedicate this home to work and leisure. May it have gaiety and high fellowship, with kindness in its voices and laughter within its walls. We light a candle to happiness.

PEOPLE: **With the help of God and our co-operation we dedicate this home to happiness.**

CHAIRMAN OF BUILDING COMMITTEE: We dedicate this home to a friendly life. May its doors open in hospitality and its windows toward other homes. We light a candle to friendship.

PEOPLE: **With the help of God and our co-operation we dedicate this home to friendship.**

MEMBER OF WOMAN'S SOCIETY PARSONAGE COMMITTEE:

We dedicate this home to co-operation. May its duties be performed in love, its furnishings bear witness that the work of others ministers to our comfort and its table remind us that God works with us for the supply of our daily needs. We light a candle to co-operation.

PEOPLE: **With the help of God we dedicate this home in the spirit of co-operation.**

MEMBER OF YOUTH FELLOWSHIP: We dedicate this home to the appreciation of all things true and good. May the books bring wisdom, the pictures symbolize things beautiful, and the music bring joy and inspiration. We light a candle to appreciation.

PEOPLE: **With the help of God we dedicate this home in the spirit of appreciation.**

MINISTER: We dedicate our time and talents to live for one another, to serve our generation and to help build

129

a world in which every family may have a home of comfort and fellowship. We light a candle to Christian service.

PEOPLE: **With the help of God and our co-operation we dedicate this home to Christian service.**

MINISTER'S WIFE: We dedicate this home as a unit in the church universal, an instrument of the kingdom of God, a place for worship and Christian training, and a threshold to the life eternal. We light a candle to spiritual enrichment.

PEOPLE: **With the help of God and our co-operation we dedicate this home to spiritual enrichment.**

HYMN: "Blest Be the Tie That Binds" (First Stanza)

DEDICATORY PRAYER AND BENEDICTION

3. BLESS THIS HOUSE [3]

Why should a home not be dedicated? Dedications are proper. We dedicate schools, churches, municipal buildings, colleges, bridges, and almost every kind of structure imaginable. We would agree that a dedication service in which some mention is made of the intended purpose of the building or object being dedicated is a most wholesome procedure.

A home surely has a definite purpose in the world and in

[3] As arranged by Dennis W. Foreman, and used in St. Paul's Evangelical and Reformed Church, Canton, Ohio.

the lives of the people of the world. In our times, when so many things happen to our homes, so many assaults are made against the life of the home from its very beginning, it might help to dedicate our homes as we take up residence in them.

The procedure is very simple. Many of our young people are either buying or building their own homes. When they move into their new place of dwelling, one of the first things they do is to have the home dedicated. The service is brief and simple. Most of the time, those participating in the service are the members of the Sunday-school class to which the young homeowners belong. Others are welcomed. The minister leads the service which follows:

General statement by the minister, dealing with the young homeowners and their relationship to the community and the church.

POEM: "It Takes a Heap O' Livin'," Edgar A. Guest [4]

> MINISTER: To the honor and reverence of Almighty God, who, through his infinite wisdom and love brought together these young people in the bonds of holy matrimony and has blest their union,
>
> PEOPLE: We dedicate this house.
>
> MINISTER: To the wholesomeness of good fellowship with this community and good neighborliness with all who live within the community which surrounds these

[4] For the text of these verses see "The Dedication of a Manse," p. 123.

walls, that all may find and give blessings to one another.

PEOPLE: We dedicate this house.

MINISTER: To the good health and happiness, comfort and well-being; to the relaxation of wearied spirit; to the restorative rest of tired flesh after honest toil when day is done; to the safety and security of all who shall henceforth be blest by the shelter of this roof and these walls,

PEOPLE: We dedicate this house.

MINISTER: To the reverence of all things good, true, and wholesome; to the beauty of simple, good, and useful living—good deeds, good thoughts, kind ministries of hands and heart,

PEOPLE: We dedicate this house.

MINISTER: To peace within, to the joy and gladness of all who may find their abode here, to the sweetness of sympathy and care, to the healing of understanding, to the refreshing of happy minds in harmonious living with one another,

PEOPLE: We dedicate this house.

MINISTER: To the bonds of Christian fellowship with other like-minded worshipers; to the propagation of our Lord's will through the good fellowship of believers; to the loyal support of his kingdom through reverence to all things holy, especially for the life and rights of our fellow men; to the promotion of the cause of justice, truth, love, peace, good will on earth, by the means of consecrating self and all possessions to God's direction,

PEOPLE: We dedicate this house.

MINISTER: To the end that all who share the hospitality of these walls and these rooms may grow in mind, spirit, joy, and happiness, that the overflow of their abundance may bless and help all who come near; and to the end that all who share the warmth and glow of the within may find courage, trust, confidence, and faith to bravely meet each tomorrow unafraid,

PEOPLE: We dedicate this house.

HYMN: Concluding verses of "Blest Be the Tie that Binds"

The hymn is usually followed by a prayer of dedication by the leader, and this followed by the company present praying the Lord's Prayer together, while all stand in a circle with hands joined.

4. LITANY FOR THE DEDICATION
OF A HOSPITAL [5]

MINISTER: In the name of the Father, and of the Son, and of the Holy Ghost.

PEOPLE: AMEN.

MINISTER: Our help is in the name of the Lord,

PEOPLE: Who made heaven and earth.

MINISTER: Our Lord Jesus said, "Come unto me, all ye that labour and are heavy laden, and I will give you rest.

PEOPLE: "Take my yoke upon you, and learn of me; for I am meek and lowly in heart: and ye shall find rest unto your souls."

MINISTER: When the even was come, they brought unto him many that were possessed . . . and he cast out the spirits with his word, and healed all that were sick:

PEOPLE: That it might be fulfilled which was spoken by Esaias the prophet, saying, Himself took our infirmities, and bare our sicknesses.

MINISTER: The Lord is nigh unto all them that call upon him, to all that call upon him in truth. He will fulfil the desire of them that fear him: he also will hear their cry, and will save them.

The Lord be with you,

PEOPLE: And with thy spirit.

MINISTER: Blest and dedicated be this building to the glory of God and the ministry of love and healing care, in

[5] Contributed by Roy D. Brokenshire, pastor, Carlsbad Union Church, Carlsbad, California.

the name of the Father, and of the Son, and of the Holy Ghost. Amen.

Inasmuch as ye have done it unto one of the least of these my brethren, ye have done it unto me.

Hallowed also be this building and the gifts there to the honor and memory of those beloved of the donors.

Bear ye one another's burdens, and so fulfil the law of Christ.

The memory of the just is blessed.

Let us pray.

O Lord God, our Heavenly Father, compassionate and merciful, who dost heal all our diseases and comfort us in all our distresses, and who dost commit thy suffering children to our loving care and ministry, be pleased to accept at our hands this building, reared in thy name to thy glory, and to be a harbor and resting place for those troubled with sickness; and of thy mercy, we beseech thee, put upon it and all that is done here to relieve and cure the distresses of body and mind thy healing benediction, so that thanksgiving may rise to glorify thee who art our health and our song; through Jesus Christ, our Savior. AMEN.

Let us pray for all who may be brought to this house of mercy.

O God, our Father, whose compassion never faileth, whose love ever guardeth, whose presence ever aideth: hear us, we humbly beseech thee, when we pray for all who may ever come here seeking health, and grant that they may find both health of body and the healing medicine of thy saving grace, through Jesus Christ, our Lord. AMEN.

Let us pray for all who minister here.

Most merciful Father, who dost commit to our love and care our fellow men in their necessities: graciously be with and prosper all those who are seeking and ministering to the sick and needy, especially those who are serving in this place. Let their ministry be abundantly blessed in bringing ease to the suffering, comfort to the sorrowing, and peace to the dying; and let their lives be inspired with the consecration of selfless service, knowing that inasmuch as they do it unto even the least of the Master's brethren, they do it unto him who came to minister thy love unto men, even thy Son, Jesus Christ, our Lord. AMEN.

Let us pray for all who in this place will cry to our Father.

Almighty and Everlasting God, the comfort of the sad, the strength of sufferers, let the prayers of those that cry out of any tribulation come unto thee, that they may rejoice to find thy mercy is present with them in their affliction; through Jesus Christ, our Lord. AMEN.

Let us pray as our Master has taught us, for each other and for ourselves.

Our Father which art in heaven, Hallowed be thy name. Thy kingdom come. Thy will be done in earth, as it is in heaven. Give us this day our daily bread. And forgive us our debts, as we forgive our debtors. And lead us not into temptation, but deliver us from evil: For thine is the kingdom, and the power, and the glory, for ever. AMEN.

5. DEDICATION SERVICE FOR A CAMP [6]

CHOIR SELECTION

PRESENTATION OF GIFTS FROM VARIOUS CHURCH GROUP TO THE CAMP

DEDICATION WORSHIP (*By the Worship Committee of the first week campers*)

CAMP CHOIR: "Camp Song"

SCRIPTURAL CALL TO WORSHIP: Ps. 107:1, 3, 7-8

HYMN: "This Is My Father's World"

LITANY DEDICATION

LEADER: Believing that God is God, indoors and out-of-doors, and that his children should know him in both places, we establish this camp. This camp is to be a home where young people and adults, living together as a family, learn, experience, and know Christian life through praying and playing.

RESPONSE: To this purpose we dedicate this camp, O Lord.

[6] As used at the Vermont Congregational Conference Camp, Wihakowi, Northfield, Vermont.

LEADER: Here, the bond that ties our local and world-wide Christian family is strengthened.

RESPONSE: To this purpose we dedicate this camp, O Lord.

LEADER: This Christian camp provides a spiritual setting which in turn promotes a Christian way of life.

RESPONSE: To this purpose we dedicate this camp, O Lord.

LEADER: Our program provides an inspiration for local church leaders.

RESPONSE: To this purpose we dedicate this camp, O Lord.

LEADER: The way of life at this camp enables Christians to study the ever-changing role of the church in society.

RESPONSE: To this purpose we dedicate this camp, O Lord.

PRAYER OF DEDICATION

Our Father, we praise thy name for all the treasured memories that enrich and ennoble our lives. Thank you for the wonderful time that we have had this week, for the friends that we have made, for sunshine and flowers, for storm clouds and starry night, for the beauty of the dawn, and the glory of the sunset, for the deep water to swim in, for hills to climb and hard work to do, for music that lifts our hearts to heaven, for the handclasp of a friend, and for the people who have made this camp possible. Rest thy blessings upon them, that in the future we will still have this camp and the opportunities it offers. May this camp which we now dedicate be an enduring witness for all the future campers and thy people. Help us to use the things we have learned so that when we go home we will be better Christians. AMEN.

6. THE DEDICATION OF A BUSINESS ESTABLISHMENT [7]

OPENING BIBLE VERSES

What doth the Lord thy God require of thee, but to fear the Lord thy God, to walk in all his ways, to love him, and to serve the Lord thy God with all thy heart and with all thy soul, to keep the commandments of the Lord, and his statutes, which I command thee this day for thy good? (Deut. 10:12-13.)

INVOCATION

STATEMENT OF PURPOSE

Today we are met in these friendly surroundings in this newly established place of business to rededicate its owner and manager to God and to give religious recognition to this business concern.

It is altogether fitting and proper that a place of business should be established. Business acumen, thrift, dili-

[7] Used by S. W. Hutton, Executive Secretary, Texas Convention of Christian Churches, Fort Worth, Texas.

gence, and honesty are worthy traits of character. The owner and manager of this business house possesses these traits of character. They are embedded in a sound Christian faith. He is active in his church. We are here today as a group of his comrades and friends to point up the significance of this forward step he has taken. We marvel at what has been achieved. We rejoice in this privilege. We congratulate our friend, _____.

SCRIPTURE READING: Rom. 8:31-39 or I Cor. 3:10-16

SPECIAL MUSIC (*by male or mixed quartet*) (*If there is a musical instrument in the building, it may be used to accompany the singers or for a special number.*)

A WORD OF COMMITMENT (*by the owner and manager of the business concern*):

This is a day of rejoicing for me and for my family, and for those who are to be associated with us in this business enterprise. We feel that except the Lord build the house they labor in vain who build it.

It is our supreme purpose to do what is good, to do what the Lord requires, to deal justly with our customers, to render kindly dealings toward everyone with whom we have contact, and in deep humility to give God the glory. We hereby commit at least one tenth of our increase to the work of Christ's church.

LITANY OF DEDICATION

MINISTER: To the end that all who enter this place of

business will sense the true spirit of brotherhood and service,

PEOPLE: **We dedicate this business concern.**

MINISTER: To growth in meeting the needs of those who deal with this place,

PEOPLE: **We dedicate this business concern.**

MINISTER: Toward the continuing spirit of friendliness, honest dealings, satisfactory service, noble business enterprise,

PEOPLE: **We dedicate this business concern and the entire personnel managing, helping, serving here, seeking to make a living in this community while keeping their own lives above reproach.**

PRAYER OF BLESSING AND BENEDICTION

Index

142

144

Date Due